A Da Capo Press Reprint Series

CIVIL LIBERTIES IN AMERICAN HISTORY

GENERAL EDITOR: LEONARD W. LEVY
Brandeis University

THE FREEDOM OF
SPEECH AND WRITING
UPON PUBLIC AFFAIRS
CONSIDERED

BY WILLIAM BOLLAN

DA CAPO PRESS · NEW YORK · 1970

A Da Capo Press Reprint Edition

This Da Capo Press edition of *The Freedom of Speech and Writing Upon Public Affairs Considered* is an unabridged republication of the first edition published in London in 1766. It is reprinted by permission from a copy owned by the Amherst College Library.

Library of Congress Catalog Card Number 75-107346

SBN 306-71878-2

Published by Da Capo Press
A Division of Plenum Publishing Corporation
227 West 17th Street, New York, N.Y. 10011
All Rights Reserved

Manufactured in the United States of America

THE

FREEDOM

OF

SPEECH and WRITING

UPON

PUBLIC AFFAIRS,

CONSIDERED;

WITH

AN HISTORICAL VIEW

OF

The Roman Imperial Laws againſt Libels, as Violations of Majeſty, or leſſer Offences.

The Nature and Uſe of Torture among the Romans and modern Europeans.

The bringing of the Rack into the Tower, where it remains, for a beginning of the Civil Laws in England.

The different Treatment of Libels there.

The Origin, legal and aſſumed Juriſdiction, Severities, Subſervience to arbitrary Power, and Abolition of the Court of Star-chamber, and of Trial by Juries.

With Obſervations on the proper Uſe of the Liberty of the Preſs, and its Abuſes, particularly of late with reſpect to the Colonies; and a brief State of their Origin and political Nature, collected from various Acts of Princes and Parliaments.

Qui non libere veritatem pronunciat, proditor veritatis eſt.

Τὐλεύθερον δ᾿ ἐκεῖνο, εἴ τις θέλει πόλει
Χρησόν τι βύλευμ᾿ εἰς μέσον φέρειν, ἔχων.
Καὶ ταῦθ᾿ ὁ χρήζων, λαμπρὸς ἔσθ᾿, ὁ μὴ θέλων,
Σιγᾷ. τὶ τάτων ἐςιν ἰσαίτερον πόλει;

Euripid. Hicetid.

LONDON

Printed; and Sold by S. BAKER, in *York-Street, Covent-Garden.*

MDCCLXVI.

THE

Freedom of Speech and Writing

UPON

PUBLIC AFFAIRS,

CONSIDERED, &c.

TRUTH is the perfect image, conception, or reprefentation of things, by which their nature, ftate, and relations, are clearly difcerned; the proper object of real knowledge, which, when attained, becomes the pure and pleafing light of the ingenuous mind. Prejudice on the other hand dignifies, adorns, debafes, deforms, and, by innumerable ways, mifreprefents for the more part the objects of our attention. By knowing all the neceffary truth, our minds being well difpofed, we are, in proportion to our talents, qualified for judgment, counfel or action, in public or private affairs. Through prejudice, the parent of ignorance and error, we miftake delufion for conviction, are mifled and miflead, fuffer and commit injuries unfpeakable and irremediable. Truth is effential to juftice and equity, which form the chief bands of fociety, the dignity of government, and the honour of human nature. Through prejudice partialities abound, the great law of confideration is daily broken, neglected or perverted, merit is fupplan ed, and artifice, weaknefs and wickednefs, take the place of wifdom and goodnefs,

nefs.   But prejudice is not the fole enemy of truth, the paffions frequently become its powerful foes, and by their various operations obftruct its progrefs. It is the office of reafon to fearch out and fupport the truth, to prevent or extirpate prejudice, to direct the paffions to their proper objects, and confine them within their proper limits ; yet how often do prejudice and paffion, fingle or united, prevail over reafon, and make it fubfervient to their domination.   All men, faid my friend *Harpocrates*, are governed by an alternation of reafon, paffion, and prejudice, or by various combinations of thefe principles of human action ; and let us furvey the globe, mark its divifions, confider their prevailing opinions, and confequent practices, and then declare, if poffible, in what proportions the whole, or any of its parts, are governed by thefe principles.   If human knowledge be found unequal to this declaration, yet I prefume we fhall clearly perceive that, in all nations, prejudice and paffion poffefs a large portion of dominion, and that the chief rulers and minifters, and the individuals of particular orders who form their refolutions, are fometimes fo far influenced by them, that grievous mifchiefs to the community, for whofe fake they were appointed, enfue thereupon ; fo that all perfons in authority have reafon to revere the faying of *Vopifcus*, occafioned by the temperate conduct of the *Romans*, during the long interregnum which took place between the death of the emperor *Aurelian*, and the election of *Tacitus*.   In order to the choice of a good prince, this author fays, that " a ftrife between the fenate and *Roman* army, not en-
" vious or fevere, but grateful and confcientious, fubfifted fix whole
" months.   How great was the concord of the foldiers, and quiet of
" the people, and how weighty was the authority of the fenate ? no ty-
" rant rofe up ; under the government of the fenate, the foldiers and the
" *Roman* people, the whole world was governed.   They did not through
" fear of any prince or tribunicial power act thus rightly ; but *(what is*
" *the beft thing in life) they feared themfelves.*"

It is the honour and happinefs of a man to delight in truth, the friend of probity and wifdom, ever exercifing a free judgment to feek her with diligence, and receive her with pleafure whencefoever fhe comes, and in whatever drefs fhe appears ; and the higher his ftation the greater honour and benefit he will receive from this difpofition.   *Darius* the fon of

Hyftafpes,

Hyſtaſpes [a], has perpetuated his fame by his conduct when he ſat in the royal ſeat of judgment, ſurrounded by all the princes of *Perſia* and *Media*, the governors, captains, lieutenants, and chief officers of his dominions, extending from *India* to *Ethiopia* ; for upon ſpecial enquiry, and hearing of advocates, whether Wine, the King, Women, or Truth, were the ſtrongeſt, when the advocate for Truth concluded his argument, ſaying, " Bleſſed be " the God of Truth," all the people ſhouted and ſaid, " Great is Truth, " and mighty above all things ;" and the king beſtowed on him the nobleſt rewards.   But although Truth, with the aſſiſtance of Time, be victorious ; yet it is certain, that in many caſes nearly affecting the welfare of individuals or ſocieties, ſhe comes not in ſeaſon, and waits ſo long to be introduced by Time in her native beauty and force, that the occaſions which called for her are paſt and gone, and ſhe ſerves only to expoſe and condemn thoſe errors and injuries whoſe conſequences cannot be avoided.   By her appearance in ſeaſon ſhe might have ſaved a perſon or a kingdom ; but by her delay ſhe becomes a ſharp accuſer, and a helpleſs friend.   And it is certain that many perſons, however well diſpoſed, are unable, without ſpecial aſſiſtance, to form in their minds a circle of all the proper relatives of a ſubject, and after placing them in their order, duly to obſerve their united force reſpecting the central point of enquiry, and that many ſubjects of laſting importance to ſocieties, by reaſon of the great number, and intricate nature of ſome, of their neceſſary parts, are not eaſily comprehended by wiſer men, even when void of prejudice and paſſion, and poſſeſſed of all their relatives ; and oftimes ſome of theſe are induſtriouſly concealed, or otherwiſe unknown, and every art is practiced to dreſs up error in the guiſe of truth. In ſhort, the difficulties that attend the acqueſt of truth are frequently ſuch that we have too much reaſon to remember the ſaying of the ancient philoſopher, ſo often repeated by others, that ſhe lies in the deep.

Truth being in its nature ſo noble, excellent, and uſeful, its enemies ſo formidable, and its acqueſt ſo difficult, the free uſe of the means of diſcovering it merits, I apprehend, our ſpecial regard.   Of theſe, it is evident, the chief are ſpeech and writing, or printing, a ſpecies of writing

---

[a] 1 *Eſdras*, Chap. iii. and iv. and *Joſephus* Antiq. B. xi. c. 3.

invented

invented for the more expeditious multiplication of copies, both being modes of prefenting to the eye what fpeech conveys to the ear; yet the right, propriety, utility, and limits of their ufe touching political fubjects, have occafioned much confideration, debate and difficulty in the world. Defpotifm cuts this matter fhort, and having fwept away all the rights and liberties of the people, prohibits and punifhes of courfe the ufe of the means of knowing the truth, which by fetting before them in full light their natural, juft, and immutable rights, together with the horrid ftate of their flavery, would confequently make them free, or at leaft indanger the quiet of that tyranny whofe exiftence fo much injures, difhonours, and debafes human nature. Under other forms of government this matter has received different treatment in different countries, and in them at different periods. I fhall not attempt to ftate thefe differences, but obferve that freedom or reftraint of fpeech and writing upon public affairs have generally been concomitant; and power being in its nature progreffive, they who are follicitous to augment the reftraints of writing would, upon their fuccefs, in all probability, proceed in like manner to reftrain liberty of fpeech; and the more injurious the defigns and actions of men are, the greater their folicitude will ever be to prevent the free examination of them; wherefore thofe who defire to preferve the latter ought by all means to take due care of the former.

After giving this matter the beft confideration in my power, it appears to me that the free examination of public meafures, with a proper reprefentation by fpeech or writing of the fenfe refulting from that examination, is the right of the members of a free ftate, and requifite for the prefervation of their other rights; and that all things publifhed by perfons for the fake of giving due information to their fellow fubjects, in points mediately or immediately affecting the public welfare, are worthy of commendation. And it being certain, that even the proper remonftrance of the moft worthy perfons, made to their prince in confequence of their refolution not to become parties to his open violation of the laws of the kingdom, hath in time paft been deemed libellous, I fhall endeavour, notwithftanding fo many excellent things faid by others upon this important fubject, a little farther to illuftrate it. All things, every one is fenfible, are beft underftood when known from their beginnings,

and

and confidered in all their relations; and it appearing to me that the opinions of many *Englifh* lawyers and others touching libels were originally drawn, in fome meafure at leaft, from a fource in general unfavourable to liberty, I mean the *Roman* Imperial laws, I fhall ftate them in the firft place.

By what laws libels in general were governed from the diffolution of the common-wealth to the time of *Conftantine* I have not been able clearly to difcover; but am much inclined to think that they fell chiefly, if not wholly, under the *Cornelian* law *De Injuriis*, made by *Cornelius Sylla*, after his overthow of the *Marian* faction, the regulation of the annual prætorian edicts, which, according to *Papinian*, were introduced for the fake of affifting, fupplying, or correcting, the *civil* law for the public utility, or the perpetual edict, compiled by *Salvius Julianus*, an eminent lawyer, fome time prætor, who, while governor of *Aquitain*, by command of the emperor *Adrian*, reduced into one body what was moft equitable in the edicts for a long time yearly iffued by the prætors; which being thus reduced, augmented, and ranged according to the order of the matters, was named the *Perpetual Edict*, becaufe the emperor would have it perpetually obferved throughout the empire, inftead of the prætors annual edicts iffued till that time. This edict being loft we have little farther knowledge of it than what may be collected from the Digefts, which make part of the *Juftinianean* body of the *civil* law, wherein are contained fundry parts of it, together with gloffes of the ancient lawyers, and among them the following.

" Dig. Lib. XLVII. Tit. 10. De Injuriis et Famosis Libellis."

" 5. Ulpianus, lib. 56. ad Edictum."

" § 9. Si quis librum ad infamiam alicujus pertinentem fcripferit,
" compofuerit, ediderit, dolove malo fecerit quo quid eorum fieret:
" etiamfi alterius nomine ediderit, vel fine nomine, uti de ea re agere
" liceret; et fi condemnatus fit, qui id fecit, inteftabilis ex lege effe
" jubetur."

" Digeft,

" Digeft, Book XLVII. Title 10.   Of Injuries and Libels."

" 5. Ulpian, in the 56th book upon the Edict."

" § 9. If any perfon hath written, compofed, or publifhed a book
" tending to defame any one, or with evil intent hath caufed any fuch
" thing to be done, although he hath publifhed it under the name of
" another, or without name, as if he might treat of that matter; if he
" be condemned, who ever hath done this, by the law is ordained to be
" inteftable."

" 15. Ulpianus, lib. 77. ad Edictum."

" § 25. Ait prætor: Ne quid infamandi causa fiat: si quis
" adversus ea fecerit, prout quaeque res erit, animad-
" vertam."

" § 27. Generaliter vetuit prætor quid ad infamiam alicujus fieri.
" Proinde quodcunque quis fecerit vel dixerit, ut alium infamet, erit
" actio injuriarum. Hæc autem fere funt quæ ad infamiam alicujus
" fiunt—aut fi carmen confcribat, vel proponat, vel cantet aliquod quod
" pudorem alicujus lædat."

" 15. Ulpian, in the 77th book upon the Edict."

" § 25. The Prætor faith, Let nothing be done for the fake of defam-
" ing: if any perfon act contrary, I will animadvert according to the
" nature of the matter."

" § 27. The Prætor generally forbiddeth any thing to be done to de-
" fame any perfon.   Confequently, whatfoever any perfon fhall do or
" fay to defame another will give an action of injuries.   And thefe are
" the things ufually done to defame any perfon,—or if he write, or
" publifh, or fing any thing that may offend another's modefty."

Julius Paulus the lawyer, who lived in the former part of the third
century, in the 5th book of his received fentences, tit. 4. § 17. fays
that " Thofe who publifhed infamous libels, to the contumely of ano-
" ther, were fubject to punifhment *extra ordinem, ufque ad relegationem*
" *infulæ,*"

" *infulæ*," by which I underſtand that they were puniſhable at the diſ-cretion of the Prætor, who might even confine them to an iſland.

The fragments of the *Gregorian* and *Hermoginian* codes, which were formed with intent to collect the conſtitutions of the emperors from *Adrian* to *Dioclefian*, make no mention of libels.

But whatever the laws relative to libels in general were that took place before the reign of *Conſtantine*, it is certain that this and other ſucceeding emperors endeavoured to ſuppreſs them by their reſcripts and edicts. The *Theodoſian* code, which was formed under the authority of the younger *Theodoſius*, compriſing the conſtitutions, with other *acta regia*, of ſixteen emperors, from the year of our Lord 312 to 438, contains the following.

IX. Cod. Theodoſ. Tit. 34. De Famosis Libellis.

" I. Impp. Constantinus A. ad Verinum Vic. Africæ."

" Si quando famoſi libelli reperiantur, nullas exinde calumnias pa-
" tiantur hii, quorum de factis vel nominibus aliquid continebunt, ſed
" ſcriptionis auctor potius requiratur; & repertus cum omni vigore
" cogatur his de rebus quas proponendas credidit, comprobare: nec tamen
" ſupplicio, etiamſi aliquid oſtenderit, ſubtrahatur. P. P. III. Kalend.
" April. Karthag. Conſtantino. A. V. & Licinio Cæſ. Coſſ. [319.]"

" II. Idem A. ad Helianum Proc. Afric."

" Licet ſerventur in officio Tuo, et vicarii, exemplaria Libellorum,
" qui in Africa oblati ſunt, tamen eos, quorum nomina continent, metu
" abſolutos ſecuritate perfrui finas; ſolumque moneas, *Ut ab omni non*
" *ſolum crimine, ſed etiam ſuſpicione veriſimili alieni eſſe feſtinent*: Nam
" qui accuſandi fiduciam gerit, oportet comprobare, nec occultare quæ
" ſcierit: quoniam prædicabilis erit ad dicationem publicam meritò per-
" venturus. P. P. V. Kal. Mar. Cathagine. Conſtantin. A. VI. & Con-
" ſtantio Cæſ. Coſſ. [320.]"

" III. Idem A. ad Januarium agentem Vicariam præfecturam."

" Ut accuſatoribus patientia præbenda eſt, ſi quem perſequi in judicio
" volunt, ita famoſis libellis fides habenda non eſt, nec ſuper his ad
" Noſtram

" Noftram Scientiam referendum, cùm eofdem libellos protinus conducat
" abolcri, quorum auctor nullus exiftit. P. P. Prid. Non. Decemb. Rom.
" Conftantino. A. VI. et Conftantio Cæf. Coff. [320.]"

" IV. Idem A. ad Dionyfium."

" FAMOSA fcriptio libellorum, quæ nomine accufatoris caret, minimè
" examinanda eft, fed penitùs abolenda : nam qui accufationis promo-
" tione confidat, liberâ potiùs intentione, quam captiosâ atque occultâ
" confcriptione, alterius debet vitam in *judicium* devocare. P. P. Tyro,
" XII. Kalend. Nov. Januarino et Jufto Coff. [328]"

" V. Imp. CONSTANTIUS A. ad Afros."

" LIBELLIS, quos *famofos* vocant, fi fieri poffit abolendis, Inclytus
" Pater nofter providit : et hujus modi libellos, *Ne in cognitionem quidem*
" *fuam, vel publicam* juffit *admitti :* Non igitur vita cujufquam, non
" dignitas concuffa his machinis vacillabit. Nam omnes hujufmodi
" libellos concremari decernimus. Dat. XIV. Kal. Jul. Urfo et Polemio
" Coff. [338.]"

" VI. Idem A. ad Populum."

" NEMO prorfùs de famofis libellis, qui ne que aput Me, neque in ju-
" diciis ullum obtinent locum, calumniam patiatur: *Nam et innocens cre-*
" *ditur, cui defuit accufator, cùm non defuerit inimicus.* Dat. Prid. Kal.
" Nov. Med. Arbitione et Lolliano Coff. [355.]"

" VII. Impp. Valentinianus, et VALENS AA. Edictum."

" FAMOSORUM infame nomen eft LIBELLORUM. Ac fi quis vel colli-
" gendos, vel legendos putaverit, ac non ftatim chartas igni confumpferit,
" fciat fe capitali fententiâ fubjugandum. Sane fi quis devotionis fuæ ac
" falutis publicæ cuftodiam gerit, nomen fuum profiteatur, et ea quæ per
" famofum profequenda putavit, ore proprio edicat : ita ut abfque ulla
" trepidatione accedat, fciens, quod fi adfertionibus veri fides fuerit opi-
" tulata, laudem maximam ac præmium a Noftra Clementia confequetur.
" Dat. XIV. Kal. Mar. Conftantinop. Valentiniano et Valente A A. Coff.
" [365.]"

" VIII.

" VIII. Idem A A. ad Florianum Com."

" JAMPRIDEM adverfus calumnias firmiffima funt præfidia comparata.
" Nullus igitur calumniam metuat : conteftatio verò, quæ caput alterius
" contra juris ordinem pulfat, depreffa noftris Legibus jaceat ; intercidat
" furor famoforum (fæpe ut conftituimus) libellorum, &c. Dat. V. Id.
" Novemb. Martianop. Valentiniano et Valente AA. Coff."

" IX. Imppp. Valentinianus, THEODOSIUS et Arcadius A A A."

" Cynegio P. P."

" SI quis famofum libellum five domi, five in publico, vel quocunque
" loco ignarus offenderit, aut difcerpat priùs quàm alter inveniat, aut
" nulli confiteatur inventum : Nemini denique, fi tam curiofus eft, re-
" ferat, *Quid legendo cognoverit.* Nam quicunque obtulerit inventum,
" certum eft ipfum reum ex lege retinendum, nifi proderit auctorem :
" Nec evafurum pænam hujufmodi criminibus conftitutam, fi proditus
" fuerit cuiquam retuliffe *Quod legerit.* Dat. XIV. Kalend. Feb. Con-
" ftantinop. Honor. N. B. P. et Evodio Coff. [386.]"

" X. Imppp. ARCAD. Honor. et Theod. A A A. Anthemio P. P."

" et Patricio."

" UNIVERSI, qui famofis libellis inimicis fuis velut venenatum quod-
" dam telum injecerint, hii etiam, qui famofam feriem fcriptionis im-
" pudenti agnita lectione non ilicò difcerpferint, vel flammis exufferint,
" vel lectorem cognitum prodiderint, ultorem fuis cervicibus gladium
" reformident. Dat. IV. Kal. Maii, Conftantinop. Arcad. A. VI. et
" Probo Coff. [406.]"

" IX. Theodofian Code. Title 34. OF LIBELS."

1. " The auguft emperour CONSTANTINE, to Verinus, lieutenant of
" Africa."

" If at any time libels be found, let not thofe concerning whofe
" actions or reputation any thing be contained in them fuffer any calumny
" thereby ; but rather let the author of the writing be fought out, and
" being

" being found be compelled, even by torture, to give proof of the
" things he has thought fit to publish ; however, let him not efcape
" punifhment though he fhould prove fomething. Given, March the
" 30th, at Carthage, the auguft Conftantine the 5th time, and Licinius
" Cæfar being Confuls. [319.] " [*b*].

2. " The fame auguft emperour to Helianus, proconful of Africa."

" Although there be kept in your office, and in the office of the
" lieutenant, copies of libels which have been prefented in Africa ; yet
" let thofe whofe names they contain enjoy uninterrupted fecurity, and
" only admonifh them that they haften to avoid not only every crime,
" but alfo probable fufpicion ; for he who hath confidence to accufe
" ought to prove, and not conceal what he knoweth ; becaufe he who
" is worthy of praife will with good reafon come to public judgment.
" Given, Feb. the 25th, at Carthage. The auguft Conftantine the 6th
" time, and Conftantius Cæfar being Confuls [320.]

3. " The fame auguft emperour to Januarius, vice prefeȼt."

" As patience is to be fhewn to accufers profecuting any perfon in
" judgment, fo no credit is to be given to libels, nor are they to be re-
" ferred to our knowledge, as fuch libels ought forthwith to be burnt
" of which there is no author. Given Decemb, the 4th, at Rome.
" The auguft Conftantine the 6th time, and Conftantius Cæfar being
" Confuls [320.]"

4. " The fame auguft emperour to Dionyfius."

" A defamatory writing which hath not the accufers name is by no
" means to be examined, but utterly deftroyed ; for he who hath confi-

[*b*] *Conftantine*, although he generally governed with clemency, was fo far capable of
cruelty, that in the early part of his reign having obtained feveral viȼtories over the *Francs* or
French, a people compofed of parts of various northern nations, who to denote their freedom
took to themfelves the name of *Francs*, and made two of their kings prifoners, he expofed
them to wild beafts in the amphitheatre ; and in the latter part of his reign he put to death
his fon *Crifpus*, an accomplifhed youth, on the falfe accufation of his mother-in-law *Faufta*,
that he had made an attempt upon her honour, whereas in truth fhe had attempted to feduce
him. After confeffing her crime, he alfo put her to death.

" dence

" dence to accufe ought by an open charge, rather than a captious and " infidious writing, to call into *judgment* the life of another. Given at " Tyre, Octob. the 21ft. Januarinus and Juftus being confuls [328.]

5. " The auguft emperor CONSTANTIUS to the Africans."

" Our illuftrious father made provifion for abolifhing if poffible thofe " writings which are called libels, and commanded that fuch kind of " writings *fhould not be admitted to the knowledge of himfelf or the pub-* " *lic.* Therefore neither the life nor dignity of any perfon battered by " thefe engines fhall be fhaken ; for we decree that all writings of this " kind be burnt. Given the 18th of June. Urfus and Polemius being " confuls [338.]"

6. " The fame emperour, to the people [of Rome.]"

" Let no perfon in any wife fuffer calumny from libels, which receive " no countenance with me, nor in judgments ; *for he is believed to be* " *innocent who hath no accufer, though he hath an enemy.* Given the " 31ft of October, at Milan. Arbitio and Lollianus being confuls [355.]"

7. " The auguft emperours Valentinian and VALENS, An Edict."

" The name of LIBELS is infamous ; and if any perfon fhall think " they are either to be retained or publifhed, and fhall not immediately " burn them, be it known to him that he fhall be capitally punifhed. " Verily if any perfon regardeth his own duty and the public welfare, " let him declare his name, and make oral publication of what he hath " thought fit to difcourfe of by a libel; fo as he may come without any fear, " knowing that if his affertions be fupported by truth, he will receive " the greateft praife and reward from our clemency. Given the 16th " of February, at Conftantinople. The auguft Valentinian and Valens " being confuls [365.]"

8. " The fame auguft emperours to Florianus."

" The firmeft defence againft calumnies hath been already procured. Let " no perfon therefore fear calumny. That objection of crime which ftriketh " at the head of another contrary to the order of law, be it depreffed by
" our

" our laws : together with it perifh the rage of libels, &c. (as we have
" often decreed.) Given the 9th of Novemb. at Martianople. The
" auguft Valentinian and Valens being confuls."

9. " The auguft emperours Valentinian, THEODOSIUS, and Arcadius,.
       " to the prætorian prefect Cynegius."

" If any perfon fhall unwittingly find a libel at home or abroad, or in
" any place, let him either tear it before another find it, or confefs the
" finding of it to no perfon. Laftly, let him relate to no perfon *what*
" *he hath difcovered by reading it,* if he be fo curious. For whofoever
" fhall communicate it when found, is certainly to be held guilty by the
" law, unlefs he fhall produce the author. Neither fhall he efcape the
" punifhment appointed for crimes of this kind, if he be convicted of
" having related to any perfon *what he hath read.* Given the 19th of
" January, at Conftantinople. Honorius and Evodius being confuls
" [386.]"

10. " The auguft emperours ARCADIUS, Honorius and Theodofius, to
        " Anthemius prætorian prefect, and of the council."

" Let all who by libels fhall caft a kind of poifoned dart at their
" enemies, and thofe alfo who having heard the fcandalous contents of
" the libel do not immediately tear or burn it, or produce the author
" when known, dread the avenging fword on their necks. Given the
" 28th of April, at Conftantinople. The auguft Arcadius the 6th time,
" and Probus being confuls [406.]"

The body of the *civil* Law, comprizing all the prior laws of the
empire, intended and ordained to remain in force, with fuch illuftra-
tions and additions as were thought requifite, compiled and eftablifhed
by the authority of the emperour *Juftinian,* befides the above citations from
the Digefts, contains what follows.

" Inftit. Lib. IV. Tit. 4. DE INJURIIS."

" Injuria autem committitur non folum cùm quis pugno pulfatus, aut
" fuftibus cæfus, vel etiam verberatus erit ; fed et fi cui convitium factum
                                                              " fuerit

" fuerit —— vel fi quis ad infamiam alicujus libellum aut carmen aut
" hiftoriam fcripferit, compofuerit, ediderit, dolove malo fecerit quo quid
" eorum fieret."

" Inftitutes, Book IV. Title 4. Of Injuries."

" Now an injury is committed not only when any perfon is beaten
" with the fift, or bruifed, or wounded with clubs; but alfo if a perfon
" be reproached, — or if any perfon hath written, compofed, or publifhed
" a libel, or fong, or hiftory to defame another, or with evil intent hath
" caufed any of thefe things to be done."

" Cod. Lib. IX. Tit. 36. De Famosis Libellis."

1. " Impp. Valentinianus et Valens, AA. Edictum."

" Si quis famofum libellum, five domi, five in publico, vel quocunque
" loco ignarus repererit : aut corrumpat prius quam alter inveniat, aut
" nulli confiteatur inventum. Si vero non ftatim eafdem chartulas vel
" corruperit, vel igni confumpferit, fed vim earum manifeftaverit, fciat fe
" quafi auctorem hujufmodi delicti capitali fententiæ fubjugandum. Sane
" fi quis devotionis fuæ, ac falutis publicæ cuftodiam gerit, nomen fuum
" profiteatur, et quæ per famofum (libellum) perfequenda putaverit, ore
" proprio edicat : ita ut abfque ulla trepidatione accedat, fciens (quidem)
" quod fi adfertionibus (fuis) veri fides fuerit opitulata, laudem maximam
" et præmium a noftra clementia confequetur. Sin vero minimè hæc vera
" oftenderit, capitali pœna plectetur. Hujufmodi autem libellus alterius
" opinionem non lædat. P. P. XVI. Kalend. Mart. *Conftantinop.* Va-
" lentiniano et Valente, AA. Coff. [365.]

" Code Book IX. Title 36. Of Libels.

1. " Edict of the auguft emperours Valentinian and Valens."

" If any perfon fhall unwittingly find a libel, either at home or abroad,
" or in any place, let him either deftroy it before another fee it,
" or confefs the finding it to no perfon. But if he do not immediately
" deftroy or burn the faid papers, but declare their contents, be it known
" to him that he fhall be capitally punifhed, as if he were the author
" of fuch crime. Verily, if any perfon regard his own duty, and the
" public

" public welfare, let him make known his name, and declare with his
" mouth thofe things which he hath thought fhould be profecuted by a
" libel, fo that he may approach without any fear, knowing certainly
" that if his affertions be worthy of credit, he will obtain the greateft
" praife and reward from our clemency; but if he do not prove fuch
" things to be true, he fhall be capitally punifhed. And a libel of this
" kind fhall not hurt the character of another. To the Prætorian prefect.
" February the 14th, Conftantinople. The auguft Valentinian and
" Valens being confuls. [365.] "

Before thefe compilations of *Juftinian* a great part of the empire of
the Weft was irrecoverably loft. Soon after his death the *Goths* making
frefh incurfions got poffeffion of *Italy*; to them fucceeded the *Lombards*.
By thefe ravages, together with the difinclination of all the old *Roman*
fubjects to preferve a body of laws which they had received with impatience from *Conftantinople*, *Juftinians* laws were totally loft in the
Weft: and in the Eaft, after continuing in force about feventy years,
they fuffered difcredit through defign of the emperour, or rather tyrant
Phocas, by whofe command they were tranflated into the *Greek* tongue,
introduced by his order into the forum as well as the fchools, inftead of
the *Latin*, the inftitutes being tranflated by way of paraphrafe. Thefe
tranflations continued in ufe about 260 years, till the time of the emperour *Bafil*, who began his reign in the year 867, from which epocha
the Learned date the fall of the laws of *Juftinian* in the eaftern empire,
the body of laws begun by this emperour, and completed by his fons *Leo*
and *Conftantine*, continuing in force till the diffolution of the empire by
the taking of *Conftantinople* in 1453. And thus *Juftinians* body of laws
loft their force in the Eaft; but in the year 1130, in the war for the
papacy, fome foldiers of the emperour *Lotharius*, in pillaging the city
Amalfi, found *Juftinians* Digefts or Pandects, which *Lotharius* fo highly
approved, that he afterwards eftablifhed *Juftinians* laws in *Germany* and
Italy. In confequence of this and other difcoveries, with the Imperial
favour and eftablifhment, *Juftinians* laws became generally known by the
Learned in all the ftates of *Europe*, and received by moft of them for their
government in different proportions, the greater part being chiefly governed

ed by them. This wonderful progrefs and admiffion of a body of laws into fo many countries wherein the legiflator had no authority at the time of their making, and which had fo long before totally loft all their force in the country wherein they were made, are frequently afcribed by authors to their great utility and excellence. Others have obferved, that thefe laws favouring the ecclefiaftics in feveral refpects, and being helpful to them to form their canon laws, the chains whereby they enflaved the *Chriftian* world, they contributed not a little by their influence to their reception, though the popes afterwards fcrupled not at their pleafure to refcind them. The illuftrious father *Paul*, in his treatife of matters beneficiary, obferves that *Gregory* the IXth, in imitation of *Theodofius* and *Juftinian*, who formed their codes for the politic of the empire, framed a politic——which began to lay the foundation, and to eftablifh the *Roman* monarchy, chiefly in beneficial matters——and that the old collectors of canons, particularly *Gratian*, made a collection of all that he accounted proper to the papal greatnefs, yet not without changes, alterations and falfifications——and it was believed by him he had raifed that authority to the greateft height it could attain unto; and for thofe times he was not miftaken. The Decretum of *Gratian* was compofed in the year 1151, and *Gregory* was created pope in the year 1227. But there was another prevailing reafon for the general reception of *Juftinians* laws, lefs noticed than its importance deferves, which was their favouring the power of princes. The author of the Hiftory of the Origin of the *French* Laws, a learned treatife firft publifhed about the year 1708, and fuppofed to have been written by the eminent monfieur *Argout*, and fince his death ufually prefixed to his Inftitutes of the *French* Laws, fpeaking of *Juftinians* law, after highly commending it for its general ufe and advantage, expreffes himfelf thus. " But it was chiefly of fer-
" vice to princes, whofe prerogative is therein extended in its full di-
" menfions, free from thofe fatal blemifhes it had fuffered in the fore-
" going ages; nay, it furnifhed them with matter to build very high pre-
" tenfions. The emperour of *Germany*, as fome doctors explained this law
" to him, had a right to univerfal monarchy, and others faid, that kings
" were abfolute emperours within their own dominions."

—— for

—— for the better underſtanding the nature of this law, I ſhall produce the following paſſages.

" Dig. Lib. I. Tit. 4. De Constitutionibus Principum."

" Ulpianus, lib. I. Inſtitutionum."

" Quod principi placuit legis habet vigorem : ut pote cum *Lege regia,*
" quæ de imperio ejus lata eſt, populus ei & in eum omne ſuum imperium
" et poteſtatem conferat. § 1. Quodcunque igitur imperator per epiſtolam
" et ſubſcriptionem ſtatuit, vel cognoſcens decrevit, vel de plano interlo-
" cutus eſt, vel edicto præcepit, legem eſſe conſtat. Hæc ſunt quas vulgo
" *Conſtitutiones* appellamus.   § 2. Plane ex his quædam ſunt perſonales,
" nec ad exemplum trahuntur : nam quod princeps alicui ob merita
" indulſit, vel ſi quam pænam irrogavit, vel ſi cui ſine exemplo ſubvenit,
" perſonam non egreditur."

" Digeſts, B. I. Tit. 4.   Of the Conſtitutions of Princes."

" Ulpian, Book I.   Of Inſtitutions."

" What pleaſeth the prince hath the force of law ; in as much as by the
" regal law made reſpecting his government the people confer on him all
" their authority and power.   1. Whatever therefore the emperour by letter
" and ſubſcription hath appointed, or hath judicially decreed, or in other
" manner declared [c], or by edict enjoined, appeareth to be law.   Theſe
" are what we commonly call *Conſtitutions*.   § 2. Of theſe ſome plainly
" are perſonal, and not to be drawn into example ; for what the prince
" hath indulged as a reward of merit, or if he hath impoſed a puniſhment,
" or given to any one unexampled ſuccour, this matter extendeth not
" beyond the perſon."

[c] The words *de plano interlocutus eſt,* which are here rendered, " in other manner de-
" clared," ſignify to take cognizance on the level ground, that is, not on the tribunal, or
judgment ſeat, but in the ſtreet, or in paſſing along, when the magiſtrate is going either to
the baths, to take the air, or to the games ; for to take cognizance from the tribunal is to
do ſo not from the level ground, but from an eminence.   And the lawyers uſe *pro tribunali*
and *de plano* as oppoſite phraſes.

" Inſtit.

" Inftit. Lib. I. Tit. 2. De Jure Naturali, Gentium et Civili."

" § 6. Sed et quod principi placuit legis habet vigorem; quum lege
" regia, quæ de ejus imperio lata eft, populus ei et in eum omne impe-
" rium fuum et poteftatem concedat. Quodcunque ergo imperator per
" epiftolam conftituit, vel cognofcens decrevit, vel edicto præcepit, legem
" effe conftat : hæc funt, quæ conftitutiones appellantur. Plane ex his
" quædam funt perfonales, quæ nec ad exemplum trahuntur : [quoniam
" non hoc princeps vult.] Nam quod alicui ob meritum indulfit, vel fi
" quam pœnam irrogavit, vel fi cui fine exemplo fubvenit, perfonam non
" tranfgreditur. Aliæ autem, quum generales fint, omnes procul dubio
" tenent."

" Inftitutes, B. I. Title 2. Of the Law Natural, of Nations and Civil."

" § 6. But alfo what pleafeth the prince hath the force of law ; in
" as much as by the regal law made refpecting his government the people
" yield unto him all their authority and power. Whatever therefore
" the emperour by letter hath appointed, or hath judicioufly decreed, or
" by edict enjoined, appeareth to be law. Thefe are what are called Con-
" ftitutions. Of thefe fome are plainly perfonal, and not to be drawn
" into example [becaufe the prince will not have it fo] for what he hath
" indulged to any perfon for his merit, or if he hath impofed a punifh-
" ment, or hath given to any one unexampled fuccour, it paffeth not
" beyond the perfon. But others being general doubtlefs bind all per-
" fons."

In this law and the luft of domination were founded all thofe exorbitant claims and extenfions of power which have wholly or nearly fwept
away all the liberties of the neighbouring ftates, without leaving in fome
the leaft appearance of thofe orders which were inftituted for their prefervation. It is an ancient as well as evident and important political
principle, that the laws of every ftate fhould be agreeable to its particular nature. Without due obfervance of this maxim the conftitution will
inevitably be changed ; and in mixed governments, when the underftanding or virtues neceffary in feafon to difcern, and with proper refolution

to

to oppofe, all accroaching power in the prince, who has the forces of the ftate in his hands, are wanting in thofe who are appointed to guard the common liberties, the declenfion of their authority will of courfe enfue ; and if by any means they unhappily become fubfervient to that domination which they ought, if poffible, to prevent, they confequently lofe the love of the people, and the refpect of the power they help to raife, and fo prepare their own annihilation, or by their continuance become a grievance inftead of a bleffing to the people. The *Roman* Imperial government was abfolute, and likewife tyrannical when the cafual goodnefs of the emperour did not prevent it. Every abfolute government is manifeftly in its nature a tyranny *in poffe* ; the temperate ufe of power may take place to day ; but a tyranny *in effe* may fucceed to-morrow : and although *Juftinians* laws might contain excellent regulations in many refpects ; yet as they were framed for the fupport of Imperial authority, being compofed and given in a ftate wherein all things concentered in the abfolute power of the prince, fo far as they related to power they were in their nature unfit for the government of limited monarchies. But when thefe laws were received, the ecclefiaftics were the chief poffeffors of what learning there was in the world ; their oppreffions were manifold, and power was the object of mutual defire in priefts and princes ; and others who fhould have laboured to prevent their general reception were probably infenfible that they were pregnant with fo great danger and mifchief, having no apprehenfions that a book pickt out of the rubbifh at *Amalfi* could poffibly introduce fuch grievous injuries to their pofterity.

This whole matter gives caufe, if it were wanted, to applaud the wifdom of thofe who have prefcribed to the members of mixed governments jealoufy, as a neceffary antidote againft that fatal difeafe arbitrary power ; and we have reafon to revere the memory of thofe who prevented a farther reception of thefe laws, which by favouring the advances heretofore made towards abfolute power would have augmented the danger of the common liberty, if not involved us in the fame ftate with our neighbours, efpecially confidering, together with the power and influence of thofe who were inclined to this reception, the progrefs which they had made.

Dr.

Dr. *Duck,* in his treatife *Of the Ufe and Authority of the* Civil *Law of the* Romans *in the Dominions of* Chriftian *Princes,* finifhed in the year 1648, and publifhed in 1653, with refpect to its ufe in *England,* in the firft place fays, " The *Englifh* have ever carefully preferved their laws, " and whenfoever in parliament attempt has been made to change them " according to the equity of the *Roman* law, though otherwife with " juftice enough, they have ever oppofed it, of which there are feveral " inftances in the journals. In a parliament under *Henry* III. when the " bifhops moved for an act to legitimate children by fubfequent marriage, " as *Juftinian* had upon good reafon appointed, as expreffed in the con- " ftitution for that purpofe, and the church had allowed the fame, " the earls and barons unanimoufly anfwered, *Nolumus leges* Angliæ *mutari,* " *quæ huc ufque ufu funt approbatæ; We will not fuffer the laws of* England, " *hitherto approved by ufe to be changed.* In the parliament under *Richard* " II. when *Thomas* duke of *Glocefter* and other nobles accufed *Alexander* " *Nevil* archbifhop of *York, Robert de Vere* duke of *Ireland,* and others " of treafon, and the common lawyers and civilians being required to " give their opinion had anfwered that the form of the accufation was " not rightly drawn, either according to the law of *England* or the *civil* " law, the earls and barons faid it was right according to the parlia- " mentary laws, and protefted they would never fuffer the kingdom of " *England* to be governed by the *civil* law of the *Romans;* and though " this might perhaps in thofe times proceed from fudden heat and " factious difpofition, yet it has been ever fince duly obferved, and all " authority and ufe of the *civil* law utterly excluded from the courts of " juftice, wherein the law of *England* is practiced."

Afterwards he fhews how far the *civil* law was introduced, and its profeffors favoured; and in particular fays, " The firft writer upon the " *Englifh* law is R. *Glanvil,* chief juftice under *Henry* II.; after him " *Henry Bracton,* likewife chief juftice under *Henry* III.; then *John* " *Britton* juftice of *England:* and under *Edward* I. *Gilbert Thornton,* " chief juftice of *England,* abridged *Bracton;* and under the fame king " an uncertain author, called *Fleta,* whom the celebrated *Selden* hath " lately publifhed and illuftrated, hath revived the buried name of " *Thornton.*" —— " Now thefe *Englifh* lawyers were excellently well " verfed

" verſed in the *civil* law, whence they have received very much for ex-
" plaining and adorning the *Engliſh* law. *Bracton* was profeſſor of the
" *Cæſarean* law at *Oxford,* and *Britton* doctor of laws ; and *Glanvil* and
" *Bracton* begin their books in the words and method of *Juſtinian* in
" the *Inſtitutes* ; and in their treatiſes often cite the teſtimonies and au-
" thority of the *civil* law for deciding the moſt weighty controverſies,
" not only in *private* cauſes, but in ſuch as relate to the *public* admini-
" ſtration ; and from king *Stephen,* for about two hundred years, till the
" time of *Edward* III. ſo great was the ſtudy of the *Roman* laws here,
" not only in the univerſities, but at the bar, that in the reports and
" judgments of cauſes, and in the pleadings of advocates, are very
" frequent quotations of the *civil* law, which *Selden* hath proved by
" many teſtimonies, in his diſcourſe upon *Fleta ;* and the profeſſors of
" the *civil* law were in ſo high eſteem in thoſe times, that under *Henry*
" II. there were ſeveral ſkilled therein, who were alſo clerks, *Simon de*
" *Pateſhull,* dean of St. *Pauls, Philip Lovell, John Manſel,* and many
" others, advanced to be judges in the ſupreme courts of juſtice."

" To be ſhort, our kings have ever caſt a favourable eye on the biſhops,
" clerks, and profeſſors of the *civil* law, preferring them generally to the
" chief offices of the government, as our hiſtorians do witneſs ; and in
" the reign of *Edward* III. all the great offices of chancellor, treaſurer,
" keeper of the privy ſeal, of the rolls, of the wardrobe, chancellor of
" the exchequer, and almoſt all other public offices were committed to
" them."——" The courts in which by the cuſtom of *England* they
" proceed by the *civil* law only, are reducible to three heads ; 1. The
" military court, under the conſtable and marſhal of *England.* 2. The
" court of admiralty. 3. All the eccleſiaſtical courts, under the arch-
" biſhops, biſhops, and archdeacons, which have all hitherto been in the
" hands of *civilians.*"

He afterwards ſets forth the numerous cauſes which are determined
in the eccleſiaſtical court by the *civil* and *canon* law, together with the
provincial conſtitutions of *Canterbury* &c. and ſays, " As to the *civil* law
" there is no diſpute, for it has been received by the conſent of all, and
" in this court is called, *the law of the land,*" adding a little after,
" among the courts of *England* wherein juſtice is adminiſtred by the
" *Roman*

" *Roman* laws, we muft not omit the privileges of our kings granted to " the two univerfities of *Oxford* and *Cambridge*." And it may be remembered that fo late as in the latter part of the reign of king *James*, and beginning of the fucceeding reign, Dr. *Williams*, while bifhop of *Lincoln*, was lord keeper; and that king *Charles* appointed archbifhop *Laud* one of the commiffioners of the treafury, and by his influence Dr. *Juxon* bifhop of *London* lord treafurer.

In juftice to the memory of the ancient writers upon the *Englifh* laws it is to be obferved that altho' their works contain many things of moment taken from the *civil* law, relative to the public adminiftration, as well as to private caufes, yet they ftudioufly tempered the power of the prince with law and equity, and even expounded thofe words of the paffage before cited from the Digefts and the Inftitutes, which ftrictly taken gave the force of law to the princes pleafure, in a fenfe very different from that which was ufually given to them by the *Greek* or *Latin* expofitors, who adhering to the letter favoured the abfolute power of the prince.

With refpect to libels, *Glanvil*, who enumerates many offences, makes no mention of them. *Bracton* in his third book, tract. *de Corona*, fol. 155, has the following words, being evidently taken, though not cited, fron *Juftinians* Inftitutes. *Fit autem injuria non folum cùm quis pugno percuffus fuerit, verberatus, vulneratus, vel fuftibus cæfus, verum cùm ei convitium dictum fuerit, vel de eo factum carmen famofum, et hujus modi*, which is the only paffage touching libels that I have feen in thofe ancient writers. *Stamford*, in his Pleas of the Crown, makes no mention of libels.

The *Scots* feem early to have introduced the *Roman* laws in a confiderable meafure for their government, in conjunction with their municipal laws, notwithftanding what is contained in the following paffage in *Buchanans* hiftory of their affairs in the year 1532. " There having been " from the earlieft times no ftated days in *Scotland* or certain place for " judging pecuniary contefts among the citizens, *John* duke of *Albany* " obtained of the pope, that an annual fum of money, fufficient to pay " the falary of a few judges, fhould be impofed on the whole ecclefiaftic " order, and each perfon affeffed in proportion to their benefice. *Gawen*
" *Dunbar,*

" *Dunbar*, bishop of *Aberdeen*, in behalf of himself and other priests,
" appealed to the pope. This controversy held from the 11th of March
" to the 24th of April, when a college of judges was established at
" *Edinburgh*. Altho' at the beginning they devised many things com-
" modiously for the equal distribution of justice the event was not
" answerable to expectation ; for as in *Scotland* there are scarce any
" laws save acts of parliaments, and the more part of those not per-
" petual, but temporary, and the judges do what they can to prevent the
" enacting of laws, the estates of all the citizens were committed to the
" determination of fifteen men, whose power is perpetual, and their go-
" verument evidently tyrannical; their sole decisions being laws."

Sir *George Mackenzie*, advocate to the kings *Charles* IId. and *James*
VIIth. in a treatise entitled, " The Laws and Customs of *Scotland* in
" matters criminal," part 1st. tit. 1st. § 3. says, " We follow the *civil*
" law in judging crimes, as is clear by several acts of parliament, wherein
" the *civil* law is called the common law."—" King *James* Vth. was so
" fond of the *civil* law, as *Boet*. observes *lib*. 17. that he made an act
" ordaining that no man should succeed to a great estate in *Scotland* who
" did not understand the *civil* law ; and erected two professions of it,
" one at St. *Andrews*, and another at *Aberdeen*."

" Tit. 30. § 5. He says," " Infamous libels, *libelli famosi*, are the
" most permanent of all injuries, and therefore are most severely pu-
" nished, and in it the offender shews more design, and therefore is more
" guilty."

" The punishment of this *delict* was of old arbitrary, *Paul*. lib. 5.
" *Sent. tit*. 4. But was made capital by the edict *Valentiniani* & *Valentis*.
" L. *unic*. C. *de fam. libel*. But *Clar*. makes it arbitrary by the pre-
" sent custom of *Europe* ; and so it is with us at present in *Scotland*,
" except where the prince is abused, or where a capital crime is alledged
" against any man ; for *eo casu* infamous libels are justly punished by
" death." " And thus *Fleming* was hanged for saying, *that he wisht*
" *that the king would shoot to dead, and die of the falling sickness*, 17 *May*
" 1615. But in this the words were maliciously spoken, for the speaker
" uttered them because he had lost a plea."

Having

Having ftated the *Imperial* laws againft libels, with the power of the princes who ordained them ; and *Conftantine* having exprefsly, and other emperours confequentially, fubjected libellers to torture, the ufual proceeding at the *civil* law againft perfons accufed of capital crimes, I fhall from the writings of others fet forth the nature of torture, apprehending that the whole will give us reafon to encreafe and preferve our regard for our mild and happy conftitution, with the exercife of thofe virtues which are neceffary in point of execution, without which it is manifeft the benefits intended by the wifeft inftitutions cannot be enjoyed.

HEINECCIUS. vol. 5. part 7. Of his " Elements of the Civil Law ac-
" cording to the Pandects."

Tit. 18. Of examinations by Torture.

" Nor is examination made by torture, in order to draw out con-
" feffion of a crime, of which there is good caufe of fufpicion [*non ob-*
" *fcuris indiciis confirmati* lefs to be reckoned among thofe things which
" are common to all public judgments, which altho' it be a frail and
" and dangerous mean has been formerly adopted by feveral nations as
" a neceffary evil. With refpect to the *Athenians* and *Rhodians* at leaft
" we have the evidence of *Cicero.* As to the people of *Germanic* ori-
" ginal it appeareth from the 4th law of the *Wifigoths*, &c."
" Whence flow axioms. 1. examination by torture properly pertained
" to fervants. 2. They were to be ufed for drawing out the truth. 3.
" When there were the ftrongeft appearances [*indiciis*] of a heinous
" crime."
" As therefore examinations by torture pertained properly to fervants,
" the reafon is obvious why they might be tortured either as delinquents
" or witneffes ; yet not againft their mafters, unlefs in crimes of treafon,
" adultery, and fome others of an atrocious nature, and why men of
" a lower degree formerly feemed to be of the fame condition, if they
" were either profecuted as criminals, or produced as witneffes."

" From

" From the fame axiom it appeareth why by our law [*d*] noble and
" honourable perfons, bifhops and prefbyters, profeffors of arts, decu-
" rions, and their children to the third decree, foldiers, and their child-
" ren of the firft degree [*e*], are exempt from examination by torture."

" And as tortures are to be ufed only for drawing out the truth, confe-
" quently 1, they are not to be exercifed upon thofe from whom there is
" no profpect of obtaining it, as mad perfons, and children. 2, nor upon
" old men, or women with child, as death might be thereby occafioned;
" and if the judge fraudently command any perfon to be tortured to
" death, he is punifhable by the *Cornelian* law *de Sicariis*; or if he hath
" done it thro' error and ignorance he is fubject to punifhment extra-
" ordinary."

" From the fame axiom the ancients inferred that order is to be ob-
" ferved in torturing feveral perfons accufed, by beginning with the moft
" fufpected, or the weaker; who therefore feem eafier to be overcome
" by pain; that a criminal convict, but not having confeffed, may be tor-
" tured refpecting the guilt of others; that tortures may be repeated, if
" it appear from new fupervening figns of guilt [*indiciis*,] that the cri-
" minal had obftinately hardened himfelf under the torture."

" Nor do we lefs hence infer that not fuch torments are to be ufed
" as the accufer requires, but fuch as are legitimate [*f*]; and that thofe
" are to be attempered by the judge according to the appearances of
" guilt in the perfon accufed, and the atrocity of the crime, left the
" mean of obtaining the truth be more grievous than the imminent pu-
" nifhment itfelf."

" Laftly, as tortures take place only where there are the ftrongeft ap-
" pearances of guilt, confequently, 1, they are not to be begun with.
" 2, they are to be ufed only on the fufpicion of a capital crime, and,
" 3, in fuch manner as that confeffion alone may feem to be wanting.
" 4, the perfon accufed firmly denying, or revoking the confeffion, and

[*d*] The law of *Pruffia*.

[*e*] But all privilege of dignity ceafeth in the greater crimes, as of rebellion and treafon,
fraud [*falfi*] poifoning, with which we fee is reckoned herefy by the principles of the heretic-
fcourgers.

[*f*] Among the torments ufed by the *Romans* were, burning, ftripes, goads, irons for the
neck or feet, collars, or yokes, pincers, cords, barbed darts, and chiefly the rack.

perferving

" perfevering therein, is to be adjudged to have cleared himfelf, and
" therefore is to be acquitted."

" *Nemefis Carolina* obferveth nearly the fame things. This only is to
" be noted, 1, that in the prefent cuftom not fo much regard is had to
" dignity. 2, that many marks [*indicia*] of crimes which feem to require
" the ufe of tortures are recounted in that *Carolina* conftitution, as well
" thofe that are general, as the fpecial, of homicide, infanticide, poifon-
" ing, theft, and rapine, burning, magic, and fortune-telling. 3, that the
" degrees of torture are at prefent for the moft part three, altho' differ-
" ent inftruments are ufed in different places. 4, fometimes, if either the
" crime be moderate, or the figns of guilt not very great, inftead of tor-
" ture, what they call *territion*, and that either *verbal* or *real*, is decreed.
" 5, that when the perfon accufed is by torments or territion brought to
" confeffion, that confeffion, after fome days, is accounted ratified, with-
" out torture taking place."

Nemefis Carolina is the conftitution of the emperour *Charles* theVth. and
of the ftates of the Sacred *Roman* empire, containing and eftablifhing the
laws in capital cafes, or the criminal conftitutions of public judgments,
declaring the duty of judges, affeffors, counfellors, fenators, and other
perfons employed in capital judgments, and directing the proceedings
againft the perfons accufed, made in the year 1532.

Among the reafons affigned for making this conftitution, it is therein
declared, that thro' the unjuft fentences of unfkilful, or crafty judges,
innocent perfons were caft into prifon, rafhly fubjected to tortures, and
even with greater boldnefs unjuftly punifhed, and that the truly guilty,
by long delay fraudulently interpofed, not without fruftration of the
accufers, and crafty elufion, efcaped juft condemnation.

Criminal appearances [*indicia*] preceding the ufe of torture are explained in the 19th chapter of this conftitution, in thefe words. " As
" often as we fhall hereafter mention *indicia*, we would have all perfons
" take notice that by us marks, figns, arguments, fufpicions not light,
" conjectures legally proved, affiftances [*adminicula*] prefumptions, and
" things of that kind, are to be underftood."

The 58th chapter declares what method is to be obferved in the ufe
of torture, as follows.

" Torture

" Torture is a horrible thing, very hurtful to the bodies of men, and
" fometimes deadly; and to which even death is almoft preferable, be-
" caufe pain, as the player faith, compelleth even the innocent to lye
" [*quod dolor, ut ait Mimus, etiam innocentes mentiri cogat*] [g] and a
" good and pious man would rather dye an hundred times than lye once,
" and by lying fin, and by finning offend God. And fo much the
" more worthy of commiferation is the condition of judges, whofe igno-
" rance for the moft part is the calamity of the innocent, agreeable to
" which that moft holy prelate and doctor of the old church *Aurelius*
" *Auguftine* hath many things, in that great work which he wrote of
" the city of God, and hath left for the perufal of pious pofterity. For
" which reafon more efpecially a meafure in torture (which we juftly
" believe to have been the invention of *Tarquin* the proud, or *Mezentius*,
" or *Phalaris*, or of fome other more cruel tyrant, tho' nothing hindreth
" us from ufing it rightly, and on proper occafion) ought to be obferved
" by the judge; who fhall diligently endeavour to attemper the torments
" in proportion to the age, fex, and ftrength of the perfons, and the na-
" ture of the cafe, ufing them more frequently, or more fparingly, more
" gently or intenfly; becaufe the tortured perfons ought to remain fafe,
" in order to their difcharge as innocent, or punifhment as guilty.
" Neither let him give credit to what the accufed utter in the midft of
" pain; but only to what they fhall declare and confefs when immedi-
" ately taken from the torture, and let it be taken in writing, as being
" what will moft contribute to the inveftigation of truth." [h].

[g] This is faid in the following verfe, *Etiam innocentes cogat mentiri dolor*, of *Publius Syrus*, a *Syrian* mimographer, who was in fo great efteem with *Julius Cæfar*, that he preferred him to *Laberius*, the chief of the *Roman* authors in compofitions of this nature.

[h] An intelligent judge for a prince on the continent informs me that this conftitution continues to be the great law of the empire in capital cafes, faving fome alterations made by the king of *Pruffia*; that being chiefly collected from the *civil* law it was received in *France* and *Spain*, as fubfidiary to their laws; and that it was alfo received, and continues now in ufe in *Denmark*: but that torture, with refpect both to the innocent and the guilty, having been found to be an uncertain mean of difcovering the truth, his *Danifh* majefty has reftrained his judges from making ufe of it without fpecial directions. And altho' the *Ruffians* were fo lately civilized; yet, according to my intelligence received from a fenfible *Ruffian* officer, they have, to their honour, fo far improved the courfe of their judicial proceedings as to exclude the ufe of torture, upon full conviction that many innocent perfons had for the fake of immediate eafe confeffed themfelves guilty.

HEIN-

HEINECCIUS. " Collection of *Roman* Antiquities illustrating jurispru-
" dence." Book IV. Tit. 18. § 25.

" As therefore upon the first pleading all things were to be confirmed
" by the accuser by testimonies, and those proofs were divided into exa-
" minations by torture, witnesses, and written depositions [*quæstiones,*
" *testes, et tabulas*] something, I think, is to be observed of each from
" antiquities. *Quæstiones* were the testimonies of servants, expressed by
" the force of torments. For the accuser was wont, as soon as the judges
" with the prætor were seated, to require the servants of the person ac-
" cused to be put to the torture. But servants might not be interrogated
" touching matters affecting the life of their master, unless in the cause
" of incest and conspiracy, and afterwards even in the cause of tributes;
" in other crimes the safety of masters was not to be put in the power of
" servants. Sometimes the servants of other persons were required for
" torture; but only singly, and with the masters permission: but he was
" not otherwise obliged to permit it than if the accuser gave security to
" pay the price of them if they expired in the torture, and the estima-
" tion of the damage if they were made worse; the servants therefore
" required to be tortured being bound to the rack, in the presence of
" the advocates, were so stretched that the poor wretches hung as it
" were from a cross, and the juncture of their bones was loosened [*ipsa-*
" *que compages ossium illis divelleretur.*] Then moreover, to encrease the
" pain, sometimes were applied heated plates, iron pincers, and other
" torments of that sort, largely described by *Sigonius* and others. The
" examination by torture being taken, and the confession of the servants
" reduced into writing, that writing was kept sealed till produced in
" judgment."

This author having, in the 335th section of his 3d book of the " Ele-
" ments of the *Germanic* Law Ancient and Modern," observed that the
custom of excruciating accused persons by torments seems to have fallen
gradually into disuse in the middle age; for no footstep thereof is to be
found in the *Saxon* or *Suevic* law, each nation seeming to be content with
the more common purgations, which they judged to be a more certain
mean of investigating the truth than dire questions; whence *Schilter*
imagined

imagined that torture at length crept into the courts of the *Germans* with the *Roman* law; on the contrary *Thomafius* and *Gribner* thought it was introduced long before that time by the clergy raging againft heretics, &c. In a note hereon he fays that " the laws of other nations who have " more facredly preferved the rights and cuftoms of their country are at " this day unacquainted with torments." adding, " *Britain* truly is a " ftranger to this butchery."

To the collections of this learned author I fhall add the following.

Digeft Book XLVIII. Tit. 18. Of examinations by Torture.

§ 9. *Marcian.* B. 2. Of public judgments.

" The emperour *Pius*, in his refcript, faid that fervants might be tor-" tured in a pecuniary caufe, if the truth cannot otherwife be found " out; which is alfo appointed by other refcripts : but torture is not " readily to be ufed in a pecuniary matter ; but if the truth cannot other-" wife be obtained than by torments, examination by torture may be " ufed ; as alfo the emperour *Severus* faid in his refcript ; examination " by torture may therefore be ufed upon the fervants of others, if the " matter require it."

Tacitus being on the 25th of Sept. 275 chofen emperour by the fenate ; as *Vopifcus* relates, he thereupon made an oration to them, wherein he declared that " he would do all things agreeably to their opinion and au-" thority, and that it therefore refted with them to command and efta-" blifh thofe things which fhould appear worthy of themfelves, worthy " of a modeft army, and worthy of the *Roman* people ;" and in the fame oration he provided that fervants fhould not be queftioned in matters touching the life of their mafters, not even in the caufe of treafon. I have not feen any mention of this conftitution in the codes of the *civil* law, and am unable to fay how long it continued in force ; but it is cer-tain that in the next century *Conftantine* ordained that no privilege of dignity fhould exempt any perfons accufed from torture in cafes of treafon.

Innumerable perfons civil and military, by reafon of their dignity, em-ployment or otherwife, were generally exempt from torture, except in

cafes

cases of treason, or other nefandous crimes; but in the reign of *Valentinian* the elder, a criminal cause pending at *Rome*, respecting an attempt to poison two considerable persons, was, by reason of the indisposition of the city prefect, committed to the cognizance of *Maximinus*, prefect of the corn. He being by nature extremely cruel, and giving ear to men of infamous lives, who named some noble persons, as having employed their dependents or others dextrous in the art of destruction, maliciously represented to the emperour that the pernicious practices of many persons at *Rome* could not be discovered or punished without using the sharper punishments. Upon this the enraged emperour, by an order, appointed that in such cases, which he blended with treason, all those whom the justice of the old law, and the constitutions of the deceased emperours, exempted from the cruel examination by torture should be subject to it when the matter so required; and encreasing the dangers he associated with *Maximinus*, appointed to act at *Rome* in the place of the prefects, a military man of low degree, and of the most savage disposition. This similar collegue, with the amplitude of his new powers, encreased the innate propensity of *Maximinus* to do mischief; and now, to the great terror of the whole city, multiplied slaughters ensued, with such cruelties, that, according to *Ammianus Marcellinus*, neither the diversity of their nature, nor their number could be comprehended. Among the sufferers one senator fell. In this state of distress and danger, by decree of the nobility, legates were sent, to entreat the emperour that punishments might not be greater than the offences, nor any senator be exposed to torments in an unusual and illicit manner; who being admitted to an audience, on their relating the preceding facts, the emperour denied that he had given the order supposed, and with some emotion said that he was reproached; upon which the questor *Eupraxius* modestly convinced him of his mistake; and by this liberty [taken by the officer whose duty it was to endite the laws] the cruel order was emended, which *Ammianus* says surpassed all examples of severity. Here the advocates for the absolute power of princes may behold some of its noblest fruit, an emperour suddenly subjecting the inhabitants of *Rome*, the mistress of the world, with the members of that senate by whose wisdom it was conquered, to tortures and death, at the discretion, that is, at the

pleasure

pleafure of two moft impious and cruel men, and doing this on the bare reprefentation of one of them.

Valentinian dying fhortly after this tranfaction, in the next year, 377, upon the petition of the *Roman* fenate, *Gratian* then alone governing the weftern empire iffued the following edict.

" Impp. Valens, GRATIANUS, & Valentinianus AAA.
" ad Gracchum P. P."

" Severam indagationem per tormenta quærendi à Senatorio nomine
" fubmovemus. Dat. prid. non. Januar. Trev. Gratiano A. iv. & Mero-
" baudo. Coff. [377.] "

" The auguft emperours Valens, GRATIAN', and Valentinian,
" to Gracchus Prætorian Prefect."

" We exempt all fenators from the fevere examination by torture.
" Given the 4th day of January at Triers. The auguft Gratian the 4th
" time, and Merobaudus being confuls [377.] "

ULRIC HUBER, in his prelections of the *Roman* and modern law. part vii. Of the Pandects B. 48. Tit. 18. Of examination by Torture.

This author, who favours this practice under certain regulations, fays, " When the accufed perfon taken out of bonds pleads his caufe it fome " times happens that his examination is appointed to be taken under tor- " ments, concerning which it is in the firft place queftioned whether it " be juft to torture perfons not convicted; and it is matter of great " wonder that almoft all nations, except the *Hebrews*, fhould have held " the affirmative, the more part of learned men, not only divines, but " alfo fome lawyers, holding the negative, and among them both my " preceptors, *Anthony Mattheus* and *Wiffenback*; and fome to avoid this " neceffity have even refufed the moft ample dignities of judges, among " whom was the illuftrious *Henry Schotan* —— and that we may have " lefs need to anfwer in order the arguments of the opponents, which " are very many and pregnant, we fhall fay that neceffity alone defend-
" eth

" eth the use of examination by torments, because otherwise the im-
" punity of crimes would be intolerable to a common-wealth, without
" which it would not have been received by so great consent of the most
" civilized nations. To this add the agreement of the city, by which
" the laws made in every common-wealth seem to be approved by
" common consent of the citizens."

This author, sect. 10, sets forth the proceedings in case of confession
made upon torture, and subsequent revocation, as follows. " If the
" accused person says in torments that he will confess, he is delivered
" from the instruments of pain, and his confession, made fitting, to the
" several articles of the fact, written in order, and credit is given to it,
" if there be nothing found in it suspicious, or having no appearance of
" truth. The custom generally used is to read over the confession about
" twenty four hours after to the accused person, and to require its rati-
" fication, as it is called. This institution is neither known to the *civil*
" law nor observed in our court [*i*] ; but if the party continue silent it is
" accounted for consent ; and if he revoke the confession, he is again to
" be subjected to torments, and if he revoke the confession then again
" made, he may be tortured the third time ; then to be acquitted."

Courts of justice are the proper sanctuary of the innocent, and this
practice, which, under the pretence of doing justice, hath so often subjected them to such grievous severities, is so remote from every thing
truly divine, that, in my opinion, its continuance under the mild dispen-
sation of the gospel in so many *Christian* states is no less the subject of
admiration than concern, as they could not avoid perceiving that it was
not permitted by the less perfect law of *Moses* ; more especially considering how long since *Christianity* had so far mollified and reformed the
dispositions and customs of its professors, that they ceased to enslave each
other when made captives in war.

Unfortunately the present does not secure the future exemption of a
people from examination under torments. The *Hebrews* while they enjoyed the full benefit of the law of *Moses*, had not, I presume, the least
apprehension of any future sufferings of this kind ; and yet they were

[*i*] The supreme court of *Friezeland*, of which this author was a member.

subjection

subjected to this cruel proceeding in the extremeft manner under *Herod* the *Great*, who fcrupled no violation of the facred law, or the ancient inftitutions of his kingdom.   On the diffentions in his family this king, *Jofephus* [k] fays, in the firft place examined by torture all whom he thought to be faithful to [his fon] *Alexander*, whether they knew of any of his attempts againft him ; but they died without having any thing to fay to that matter.   After this, through the inftigation of his fon *Antipater*, he put great numbers to the torture, to difcover what attempts were ftill concealed ; and only gaining from one of them an account of matters that were either of no great moment, or improbable, and being very follicitous to obtain better evidence of his fons wickednefs, that he might not appear to have imprifoned him too rafhly, he tortured the principal of *Alexanders* friends, and put not a few of them to death, without getting any of the things out of them which he fufpected.

Waving farther particulars, it may fuffice to fay that the cruelty and wickednefs of this tyrants court brought the whole into fuch a calamitous ftate, that, having forfaken the law, which was the common fafety, there was no room for defence or refutation in order to the difcovery of the truth ; but all were at random doomed to deftruction ; fo that fome lamented thofe that were in prifon ; fome thofe that were put to death, and others lamented that they were in expectation of the fame miferies ; and a melancholy folitude rendered the kingdom deformed, and quite the reverfe to that happy ftate it was formerly in.

" Montaigne [l] has the following paffage on this fubject. " Tor-
" ture is a dangerous invention, and feems rather a trial of patience than
" of truth ; and he that can bear, and he that cannot bear it, equally con-
" ceals the truth ; for why fhall pain make me rather confefs what is,
" than force me to fay what is not ? and, on the contrary, if he that has
" not committed the fact of which he is accufed is patient enough to
" fuffer thefe torments, why will not he be fo that has, when fo great a
" reward as life is propofed to him ? I believe that the foundation of this
" invention was owing to the confideration of the effort of confcience ;
" for to the guilty it feems to aid the torture to make him confefs his

[k] Antiq. Book xvi. chap. 8.   [l] Effays, Book ii. chap. 5.

" crime,

" crime, and that it weakens him; and on the other hand to fortify the
" innocent againſt it. To ſpeak the truth, it is a method full of uncer-
" tainty and danger; for what would not a man do, or ſay, to avoid
" ſuch intolerable pains ? *Etiam innocentes cogit mentiri dolor. Publ. Syr.*
" verſ. 191. Whence it happens that he whom the judge has tortured
" to prevent his dying innocent cauſeth him to dye both innocent and
" tortured. Thouſands and thouſands have loaded themſelves with falſe
" confeſſions, among whom I place *Philotas*, conſidering the circum-
" ſtances of *Alexanders* perſecution againſt him, and the manner of his
" torture. But however, ſay they, it is the leaſt evil that human weak-
" neſs could invent; very inhuman however, and, in my opinion, very uſe-
" leſs. Several nations, leſs barbarous in that reſpect than the *Greeks* or
" *Romans* who called them ſo, held it horrible and cruel to torment and
" tear a man in pieces for a crime of which you are ſtill in doubt; what
" can it be but the effect of your ignorance ? are you not unjuſt, who
" rather than put him to death unjuſtly torture him worſe ? Let it be
" ſo; ſee how often he had rather dye without a cauſe than to undergo
" this ſcrutiny, which is more painful than the puniſhment, and often
" by its ſeverity antedates both the puniſhment and execution."

GROTIUS, in one of his letters, ſays, " That there are numberleſs
" examples of people who have been put to death unjuſtly, upon a
" confeſſion extorted from them by the rack;" adding, " that he does not
" wonder that there have been grave perſons of opinion that *Chriſtians*
" ought not to make uſe of torments, to effect confeſſion of crimes,
" ſince it is certain there is nothing like it in the law of *Moſes*; that in
" *England* they live in as great ſecurity as elſewhere, tho' examination
" by torture is not uſed there ; and that while *Rome* preſerved her liberty,
" no citizens could be put to the torture." —— *Auguſtus* violated the
right of exemption of the *Roman* citizens from torture by this deteſtable
proceeding. According to the faithful *Suetonius*, ſuſpecting that Q.
Gallius the prætor, who when ſaluting him held double writing-tables
under his robe, hid a ſword, nor preſuming immediately to ſearch, leſt
a different thing ſhould be found, a little after, being dragged by centu-
rions and ſoldiers from the tribunal, he tortured him in a ſervile manner,
and confeſſing nothing, ordered him to be put to death, having firſt dug

out

out his eyes with his own hand: of whom neverthelefs he writes that he would have infnared him by petitioning a conference, and that being by his order taken into cuftody, and afterwards difcharged, being interdicted the city, he had perifhed by fhipwrack, or by robbers.

Lord *Coke*, in the 2d chapter of his 3d Inftitute, fhewing how prifoners committed for treafon, or any other offence, ought to be demeaned in prifon, cites, *Bracton*, *Britton*, *Fleta*, and the *Mirrour*, to prove that they are to be fafely kept, not punifhed, nor conftrained to anfwer but at their free will, nor put to any pain before they be attainted, after which he writes thus.

" Hereupon two queftions do arife, when or by whom the rack or
" brake in the tower was brought in."

Rot. Par.
26 H. VI.

" To the firft, *John Holland* earl of *Huntingdon*, was by king *Hen.*
" VI. created duke of *Exeter*, and anno 26 *Hen.* VI. the king granted
" to him the office of the conftablefhip of the tower: he and *William*

Rot. Par.
28 H. VI.
nu. 30.

" *de la Poole* duke of *Suffolk*, and others, intended to have brought in
" the *civil* laws. For a beginning whereof the duke of *Exeter*, being
" conftable of the tower, firft brought into the tower the rack or brake,

Hollinfhed
pag. 670,
&c.
Innocentem cogit mentiri dolor.
Fortefcue
ca. 22.
fol. 24.

" allowed in many cafes by the *civil* law: and thereupon the rack is
" called the duke of *Exeters* daughter, becaufe he firft brought it thither."

" To the fecond upon this occafion, Sir *John Fortefcue*, chief juftice
" of *England*, wrote his book in commendation of the laws of *England*,
" and therein preferreth the fame for the government of this country
" before the *civil* law; and particularly that all tortures and torments of
" parties accufed were directly againft the common laws of *England*,
" and fheweth the inconvenience thereof by fearful example, to whom
" I refer you, being worthy your reading. So as there is no law to
" warrant tortures in this land, nor can they be juftified by any prefcrip-
" tion, being fo lately brought in."

" And the poet in defcribing the iniquity of *Radamanthus*, that cruel
" judge of hell, faith,"

Virgil.

" *Cafligatque, auditque dolos, fubigitque fateri.*"

Luke xvi.
1, 2. &c.
John vii.
51. Nun-

" Firft he punifhed before he heard, and when he had heard his denial,
" he compelled the party accufed by torture to confefs it. But far other-
" wife doth Almighty God proceed *poftquam reus diffamatus eft.* 1. *Vocat.*
" 2. *In-*

" 2. *Interrogat.* 3. *Judicat.* To conclude this point, it is against
" *Magna Carta,* cap. 29. *Nullus liber homo, &c. aliquo modo destruatur,*
" *nec super eum ibimus, nec super eum mittemus, nisi per legale judicium*
" *parium suorum, aut per legem terræ.* And accordingly all the said
" ancient authors are against any pain or torment to be put or inflicted
" upon the prisoner before attainder, nor after attainder, but according to
" the judgment. And there is no one opinion in our books, or judicial
" record (that we have seen and remember) for the maintenance of
" tortures or torments, &c."

quid lex nostra judicat hominum nisi prius audierit ab ipso?

The 27th Title of the second part of the aforementioned treatise of
Sir *George Mackenzie* is as follows.

" Of Torture."

" 1. By whom can torture be inflicted in our law.
" 2. Torture purges all presumptions.
" 3. Whether may persons who are condemned, be thereafter tortured.
" 4. Who are exeemed from torture.
" 5. How should such be punished who torture unjustly.

I. " TORTURE is seldom used with us, because some obstinate persons
" do oft times deny truth, whilst others who are frail and timorous con-
" fess for fear what is not true. And it is competent to none, but to the
" council or justices, to use torture in any case ; and therefore they found
" that Sir *Wm. Ballenden,* as a captain, could not torture, tho' it was
" alleged that this was necessary sometimes for knowing the motions of
" the enemy, and might be necessary and allowed in some cases to soldiers
" for the good of the common-wealth. And the council are so tender
" in torture, that tho' many presumptions were adduced against *Giles*
" *Thyre* Englishman, suspected of murder and adultery, they refused to
" torture him, albeit it was prest zealously by his Majestys advocate."

II. " IT is a brocard amongst the doctors, that he who offers to
" abide the torture purges all other presumptions which can be ad-
" duced against him ; and yet *Alexander Kennedy* being pursued for forg-
" ing some bonds, and nothing being adduced for proving the crimes,
" save presumptions, offered to abide the torture ; but this was refused."

" TORTURE

" Torture likewife being adduced purges all former prefumptions
" which preceeded the torture, if the perfon tortured deny what was
" objected againft him : but yet he may be put to the knowledge of an
" inqueft upon new prefumptions, as was found after a learned debate in
" the cafe of *Tofhoch*, who was tortured for the alledged burning the
" houfe of *Frendraught*, Auguft 1632 : for it was alledged, that torture
" is intended for bringing the verity to light, and as he had been con-
" demned if he had confeffed, fo he fhould be affolied when he denies,
" elfe no man would endure the torture, if they were not perfuaded that
" upon denial they fhould be cleared, but would confefs, and not endure
" fo much torment unneceffarily ; fo that the inquifition would be the
" occafion of much fin, and make men die with a lie in their mouh :
" and therefore torture is called *probatio ultima, vid. Clar. quæft.* 64. Yet
" *Spot, Maxwel* of *Garrery*, and others, were condemned after torture,
" upon other probation than was deduced before the torture."

III. " I remember it was debated in council, *anno* 1666, if the weft-
" country men who were condemned for treafon, might after fentence be
" tortured, for clearing who were their complices ; and it was found that
" they could not, *nam poft condemnationem judices functi funt officio* ; yet all
" lawyers are of opinion, that even after fentence, criminals may be tor-
" tured for knowing who were the complices."

IV. " One of the privileges of minors is, that they cannot be fub-
" jected to torture, left the tendernefs both of their age and judgment
" make them fail, ὁ ἥτ]ων τῶν δεκατισσάρων ἐτῶν ἐχ ὑφίςαται ἐμβάσανον ζήτησιν,
" *Eclog. de quæft. cap.* 9. *ad.* Yet L. 5 *ff. de quæft.* Judges are difcharged
" only to torture fuch as are under fourteen. Perfons very old were not
" to be tortured, for the fame reafon. L. 3. *ff. ad S. C. Sillan.* which was
" by fome extended to women, fick perfons, and fuch as had been emi-
" nent in any nation for learning or other arts ; but all this is arbitrary
" with us."

V. " These who torture, if the perfon tortured die, are punifhable
" as murderers ; but tho' they die not, yet by the civil law they were
" punifhed *deportatione in infulam,* or by banifhment ; and with us they
" are punifhed according to the quality of the crime."

The

The union of the kingdoms of *England* and *Scotland* was attended, among others, with this happy circumstance, the principal or greater kingdom, which of course would, and of right ought to, have its proportionate just influence over the whole, enjoyed the more mild and excellent constitution, the benefits whereof would probably be by degrees communicated to the other kingdom on their union. Accordingly we find that by an act of parliament for improving the union of the two kingdoms, passed in the 7th year of the reign of queen *Anne*, it was enacted, " that from and after the first day of July 1709 no person ac-" cused of any capital offence or other crime in *Scotland* should suffer, " or be subject or liable to any torture," to which the *British* subjects residing in that part of the united kingdom were liable from the first day of May 1707, when the union took place, in consequence of the provision thereby made for continuing the laws of *Scotland* in force.

In order to complete the enquiry into the *Imperial* laws against libels we shall in the next place consider those laws and proceedings of the emperours which respected such writings, words and actions as reproached them, or those who were arranged with them, which being blended with the greatest crimes against the state were deemed violations of majesty, or treason. *Tacitus* says, " this law in former times had the same " name; but different offences were the subjects of it, as betraying an " army, raising seditions, or lessening the majesty of the *Roman* people " by the male administration of their affairs; actions were punishable, " but words were free." and that *Augustus*" [whose conduct was well adapted to fix the fetters on a free people] " was the first who treated " libels as offences against this law, being provoked by the licentiousness " of *Cassius Severus*, who by his petulant writings had defamed illustri-" ous persons of both sexes," and artfully taking occasion thence, as some suppose, to preserve his own character free from those censorious writings for which he had given so great cause. This extension of the law of violated majesty was accompanied with the most dangerous provision; for to encrease the number of the accused even infamous persons, and servants, with freed men, were admitted to accuse; but the chief offenders only against this law were put to death, the others being punished with less severity. Afterwards, as *Tacitus* relates, this law was

revived

revived by *Tiberius*. *Pompeius Macer* the prætor confulting him whether procefs fhould be granted upon it, he anfwered that " the laws muft be " executed." He was likewife exafperated by fatyrical verfes of unknown authors, reflecting on his cruelty, pride, and want of affection to his mother. This dark tyrant for fome time diffembled his cruel difpofition fo far, that, according to *Suetonius*, " unmoved by reproaches, evil re- " ports, and lampoons, he would thereupon fay, that *in a free city the* " *mind and tongue ought to be free*." Yet after fome time, the malignity of his nature breaking thro' all difguife, he not only revived the fevere law of *Auguftus*; but extended it fo far that thefe things were treated as capital offences ; to have killed a flave, or changed a garment, near a ftatue of *Auguftus*, or to have carried that emperours image impreffed on a coin or ring into an indecent or infamous place, or to have injured any expreffion or action of his by any mifconftruction. The punifh- ment appointed by *Auguftus* did not fatisfy his cruel fucceffors ; for *Paul* the lawyer, in his received fentences, writes that in his time the lower fort were caft to beafts, or burnt alive ; the better fort were capitally punifhed. Death itfelf did not exempt perfons from accufation, and confifcation of their eftates ; and the emperours *Arcadius* and *Honorius*, influenced by their tyrannic minifters *Ruffinus* and *Eutropius*, whofe vices were the fubjects of *Claudians* invectives ; but the force of whofe lan- guage, without difparaging the poet, was far from being equal to their enormities, extended the feverities of the law of violated majefty ftill farther ; fo that the fons of perfons convicted were excluded from the inheritance of their mothers, and of all their relations, and difabled to take any thing by will from ftrangers, or to afpire to any honours ; fo that paternal infamy perpetually accompanying their poverty their life was a burthen.

J. F. Gronovius has the following note, applauded by others, on thefe words of *Tacitus* ; *facta arguebantur, dicta impunè erant*, which we have rendered, actions were punifhable ; but words were free. " Thefe " words are moft true, which the whole title in the *Digeft* on the *Julian* " law of Majefty teacheth and demonftrateth, that even after fo many " ages, fo many tyrants did not dare openly to enact that words fhould be " punifhable, tho' they fuffered the law to be wrefted by interpretation to that effect."   It

It is impoffible, in my opinion, to afcertain the feveral portions of time wherein the reproaches of the prince by words or writing were and were not confidered and profecuted as treafon. Grave authors have not fcrupled to fay that many of the *Roman* emperours were not men, but wild beafts in human fhape; and if through the goodnefs of one or feveral fucceeding emperours this wrefted law lay quiet, yet, like a fleeping lion, it was ready to be rouzed for deftruction, as foon as the caprice and ferocity of a brutal fucceffor fhould dictate; and one inftance of Imperial butchery frequently gave occafion for other feverities. Mankind are fo formed that they cannot in fome cafes forbear complaints and lamentations; and yet *Arnobius,* an *African* writer in the 3d. century obferves that the *Romans* held thofe to be guilty of treafon who in plaintive accents uttered any thing amifs of their kings [*m*], who fometimes interdicted even near relations to bewail thofe that were capitally punifhed.

After boholding fo many fcenes of horror and diftrefs we fhall at length be relieved by the fight of a few objects of a different nature. *Xiphilin* has tranfmitted to pofterity the fenfe which the moft excellent *Titus* had of the cenfures of his conduct, in his own remarkable words. After giving inftances of the emperours great clemency this author relates that judgments of impiety he neither profecuted himfelf nor fuffered others, faying, " I can indeed neither be injured nor afperfed, for I neither do any thing " worthy of reprehenfion, nor regard what is fpoken falfely."

Tacitus, after complaining that hiftorical truth was much impaired and corrupted by the eftablifhment of *Imperial* power, rejoices in the rare felicity of the times wherein he wrote, in which *it was lawful for every one to think what they would, and to fay what they thought.* Such was the freedom enjoyed under the illuftrious *Trajan,* who enlarging the empire in the Eaft and the Weft, had a more extenfive command than any other *Roman,* and whofe mind was equal to this wide dominion, with all its cares. *Aurelius Victor,* an author of the 4th. century, probably an *African,* who by his fole merit from low eftate was raifed by degrees to the confular dignity, in his account of this emperour, informs us that his adminiftration of the common-wealth was fuch, that the moft confummate writers with their utmoft efforts could fcarce defcribe its excellence;

[*m*] Majeftatis funt apud vos rci, qui de veftris fecus obmurmuraverint aliquid regibus. Adv. Gentes. lib. iv.

and, among other things, that juftice and divine and human rights were the fubjects of his wife counfels and fpecial protection.

The codes of the *civil* law make no mention of thefe regulations of two emperours whofe amiable deportment virtues and abilities were the delight, admiration and fecurity of the *Roman* world.

We fhall in the next place fet forth a notable edict of *Theodofius* the *Great*, of which *Francis Baldwin*, a lawyer in the 16th. century, famous in *France* and *Germany* for his general learning, as well as knowledgein jurif-prudence, gives this hiftorical account, in the 2d. book of his commentary on the laws of *Conftantine* the *Great*. " Concerning the crime of violated " majefty, refpecting which other princes, being fevere judges in their " own caufe, made fo many laws, we have no law of *Conftantine*; but " he hath left us an illuftrious example of his fingular clemency herein, " which is moft worthy of our remembrance. It is, to my great furprize, " indeed omitted by thofe who have in other refpects heretofore written " fuch long commentaries of *Conftantine*, either thro' negligence or for-" getfulnefs : but in reading the fermons of *Chryfoftome* preached to the " people of *Antioch*, I luckily met with that remarkable paffage whence I " have taken this ftory. Certain feditious or petulant perfons had thrown " ftones at a ftatue of *Conftantine*. They were accufed. The accufers, " the more to inflame the prince to revenge, magnified the atrocious in-" jury by the moft atrocious words, declaring with vehemence that this " violation of majefty was no lefs flagitious than if the living face of the " emperour himfelf had been ftricken and bruifed with ftones. Hereupon " *Conftantine* feeling his face with his hand, and gently fmiling, pleafantly " anfwered that he felt no wound from that ftoning. By which anfwer " he not only repulfed thofe accufers, but taught other princes, no lefs " than if he had made a law, to be placable in their own caufe. Alfo " when afterwards certain perfons at *Antioch* had thrown down the " ftatues of the emprefs *Placidia*, and *Theodofius*, being incenfed by fuch " an injury done to his wife, intended to deftroy the city [*n*], *Flavianus*,

[*n*] *Antioch*, the capital of *Syria*, according to *Chryfoftome*, was at this time the firft city of the world, whofe inhabitants, after many of them had fuffered for the fedition wherein the *Imperial* ftatues were overthrown, by fire, by being caft to wild beafts, and by the military fword, which fpared none by reafon of their tender age, continued in the utmoft dread of extirpation.

bifhop

" bifhop of *Antioch* being fent to appeafe him, particularly fet before him
" what I have related of *Conftantine*, and fo pacified *Theodofius* by that
" example, that he even publifhed a law by which he adjudged thofe to
" be pardoned who fhould have reproached the emperour." Which law
is as follows.

IX. Cod. Theodof. Tit. IV.

" THEODOSII M. *conftitutio, de* MALEDICTIS *in principem,
ejufve Tempora jactatis.*"

" Imppp. THEOD. Arcad. & Honor. A. A. A. Rufino P. P."

" SI quis, modeftiæ nefcius, & pudoris ignarus, improbo petulantique
" maledicto nomina noftra crediderit laceffenda, ac temulentiâ turbulen-
" tus obtrectator temporum fuerit, eum pœnæ nolumus fubjugari, neque
" durum aliquid nec afperum fuftinere; quoniam, fi id ex levitate procef-
" ferit contemnendum eft: fi ex infaniâ, miferatione digniffimum: fi ab in-
" juriâ, remittendum. Unde integris omnibus, ad noftram fcientiam
" referatur, ut ex perfonis hominum dicta penfemus, & utrum præter-
" mitti, an exquiri debeat, cenfeamus. Dat. V. Id. Aug. Conftantinop.
" Theod. A. III. & Abundantio V. C. Cofs. [393.]"

" A conftitution of THEODOSIUS the Great, refpecting opprobrious
" words ufed againft the prince, or his times."

" The Augt. Emprs. THEODOSIUS, Arcadius and Honorius,
" to Rufinus. Prætorian Prefect."

" If any perfon, void of modefty and fhame, fhall think our name is to
" be abufed by infolent reproach, and be wantonly a turbulent difparager

Their prefent condition was deplorable, but if the intended order of excifion had been iffued
as fuddenly as the order of *Valentinian* refpecting the inhabitants of *Rome* this noble city muft
have been utterly deftroyed, and its numerous inhabitants fubjected to calamities exceeding
all defcription.

" of

" of the times, we will not have him fubjected to punifhment, nor fuftain
" any hardfhip or feverity, becaufe if it hath pro eeded from levity it is to
" be contemned; if from infanity, moft worthy of compaffion; if from in-
" jury, it is to be pardoned. Wherefore let the whole be referred to our cog-
" nizance, that from the quality of the men we may confider the expref-
" fions, and judge whether they ought to be pardoned, or examined into.
" Given the 28th. of July, at Conftantinople. The Auguft Theodofius
" the 3d. time, and the moft noble Abundantius being confuls. [393.]"

" This conftitution was adopted by *Juftinian*, and makes part of his
" code, ftanding fingle there, and in the *Theodofian* code: but although
" clemency is allowed to be one of the brighteft jewels in the royal dia-
" dem, yet I do not perceive that any of the *European* princes, who have
" fo far received the *civil* law of the *Romans* for their government, have
" admitted this conftitution.

For the farther illuftration of the fpirit of the *Imperial* laws it may be
obferved that they were unfavourable to religious as well as civil liberty.
The *Theodofian* code contains fixty fix conftitutions againft heretics; one
of them defines heretics to be thofe, *qui vel levi argumento a judicio Catho-
licæ religionis & tramite detecti fuerint deviare;* " who fhall be difcovered
" to deviate from the judgment and path of the Catholic religion, even
" in a flight article," according to *Gothofreds* clear fenfe of this defini-
tion. Thefe conftitutions impofed on various heretics the following refpective punifhments, to wit, The doctors teaching their faith were to be
feverely fined; to be expelled the cities, and banifhed. Sometimes all
their effects were to be confifcated; fometimes they were to be fined ten
pounds of gold, together with the managers of their affairs, and thofe
who fupplied them with places to meet in; if poor, that fine was to be
levied on the common body of the clergy, or taken from the offerings:
fometimes they were to be beaten with lead, and, to diffolve their fociety,
to be fent fingly into feparate countries. The lands, houfes, dwellings,
and places (which ufually belonged to great men) in which the heretics
met and celebrated their rights, with the owners knowledge, were either
confifcated, or given to the church and clergy; alfo tenants, ftewards,
agents, and countrymen fuffering thefe affemblies were fubjected to various
punifhments; fometimes to death. All catholics were empowered to
difturb the meetings of heretics. Thofe who partook, and were privy to
their

their superstition were punished in like manner with the authors. Sometimes heretics were subjected to infamy by public edicts; odious names were given to them; they were not permitted to partake of the laws and customs of their country in common with others. The right of disposing of their estates by will to each other, and of receiving legacies, was taken away, and likewise the right of contracting, buying and selling. Some of them were sometimes commanded to be driven from their habitations, cities and provinces; from all places; from the society of honest persons, and from the communion of saints. There was no standing law for punishing heretics in general with extreme punishment; but in certain cases it was ordained that they should be put to death; and sometimes those who revived noxious books were commanded to be capitally punished. To these severities were heretics subjected, with various others respecting them and their families.

Here we have the origin of those severe laws and proceedings which for so many ages have taken place among *christians*, in consequence of their differing in opinion from each other upon religious subjects, transgressing the equal and perpetual law of doing that unto others which they would have done to themselves, whereby such manifold distress and grievous destruction have so often deformed the *Christian* world; and a view of the preceding matters, besides giving us other information, will enable us to judge in some measure of the propriety and justice of those exuberant praises which several *English* authors have indiscriminately bestowed on the *civil* law; one of whom [o], without citing others, says, " the *civile* " law is the law which the old *Romans* used, and is for the great wisdom " and equity thereof, at this day, as it were the common law of all well " governed nations, a very few only excepted. And certainly, albeit " sundry other nations by the light of nature have many rules and max- " imes in the *civile* law; yet, if all the constitutions, customes, and laws of " all other people and countries were put together, (I except none, save " the laws of the *Hebrews*, which came immediately from God) they are " not comparable to the law of the *Romans*, neither in wisdom nor equity, " neither in gravity nor in sufficiency."

[o] Dr. *Ridley*, in his " View of the Civile and Ecclesiastical Law.

Having

Having ftated the *Imperial* laws and proceedings touching libels, we fhall now confider their treatment at particular times in *England*——Lord *Coke*, in his 3d. Inftitute, has a chapter in thefe words, " Of Libels and " Libellers. What a libel is, how many kinds of libels there be, who " are to be punifhed for the fame, and in what manner, you may read " in my reports, viz. lib. 5. fo. 124, 125. lib. 9. fo. 59. To thefe you " may add two notable records. By the one it appeareth that *Adam de* " *Ravenfworth* was indicted in the kings bench for the making of a libel " in writing in the *French* tongue, againft *Richard of Snowfhall*, calling " him therein, *Roy de raveners*, &c. Whereupon he being arraigned " pleaded thereunto not guilty, and was found guilty, as by the record " appeareth. So as a libeller or a publifher of a libel committeth a public " offence, and may be indicted therefore at the common law."

Mich. 10. E. 3. coram Rege. Rot. 92. Eborum.

" *John de Northampton* an attorney of the kings bench, wrote a letter " to *John Ferrers*, one of the kings counfel, that neither Sir *William Scot*, " chief juftice, nor his fellows the kings juftices, nor their clerks, any " great thing would do by the commandment of our lord the king, nor " of queen *Philip*, in that place, more than of any other of the realm ; " which faid *John* being called, confeffed the faid letter by him to be " written with his own proper hand. *Judicium curiæ. Et quia prædictus* " *Johannes cognovit dictam literam per fe fcriptam Roberto de Ferrers, qui* " *eft de concilio regis, quæ litera continet in fe nullam veritatem : prætextu* " *cujus dominus rex erga curiam & jufticiarios fuos hic in cafu habere poffet* " *indignationem, quod effet in fcandalum juftic' & curiæ. Ideo dictus* Jo- " hannes *committitur Marefc', & poftea invenit* 6 *manucaptores pro bono* " *geftu.*" Judgment of the court. " And becaufe the aforefaid *John* " hath acknowledged the faid letter by him written to *Robert de Ferrers*, " who is of the kings counfel, which letter containeth in it no truth ; " by means whereof the lord the king towards the court and juftices in " this cafe might have indignation, which would be to the fcandal of " the juftices and the court. Therefore the faid *John* is committed to " the marefchal, and afterwards he found fix fureties for his good beha- " viour."

Mich. 18. E. 3. coram Rege. Rot. 151. Libellum.

The cafes referred to by lord *Coke*, and which, according to his declared fenfe of them, formed a body of laws refpecting libels, ftand thus in his reports.

                 " *The*

" *The case* de Libellis famosis; *or of* Scandalous Libels."

" Pasch. 3 Jacobi 1."

" In the case of L. P. in the *Star-Chamber* this term, against whom
" the attorney general proceeded *ore tenus* on his own confession, for com-
" posing and publishing an infamous libel in verse, by which *John* arch-
" bishop of *Canterbury* (who was a prelate of singular piety, gravity
" and learning, now dead) by descriptions and circumlocutions, and not
" in express terms; and *Richard* bishop of *Canterbury* who now
" is, were traduced and scandalized: In which these points were re-
" solved:
" 1. Every libel (which is called *famosus libellus, seu infamatoria scriptura,*)
" is made either against a private man, or against a magistrate or public
" person. If it be against a private man, it deserves a severe punishment;
" for altho' the libel be made against one, yet it incites all those of the
" same family, kindred or society to revenge, and so tends *per consequens*
" to quarrels, and breach of the peace, and may be the cause of shedding
" of blood, and of great inconvenience: if it be against a magistrate, or
" other public person, it is a greater offence; for it concerns not only the
" breach of the peace, but also the scandal of government; for what
" greater scandal of government can there be than to have corrupt or
" wicked magistrates to be appointed and constituted by the king to
" govern his subjects under him? And greater imputation to the state
" cannot be than to suffer such corrupt men to sit in the sacred seat of
" justice, or to have any medling in or concerning the administration of
" justice.
" 2. Although the private man or magistrate be dead at the time of
" the making of the libel, yet it is punishable; for in the one case
" it stirs up others of the same family, blood, or society to revenge, and
" to break the peace, and in the other the libeller traduces and slanders
" the state and government, which dies not.
" 3. A libeller (who is called *famosus defamator*) shall be punished either
" by indictment at the common law, or by bill, if he deny it, or *ore
" tenus* on his confession, in the *Star-chamber*, and according to the qua-
" lity

" lity of the offence he may be punished by fine or imprisonment; and
" if the case be exorbitant, by pillory and loss of his ears."

" 4. It is not material whether the libel be true, or whether the party,
" against whom it is made, be of a good or ill fame; for in a settled state
" of government the party grieved ought to complain for every injury
" done him in an ordinary course of law, and not by any means to re-
" venge himself, either by the odious course of libelling, or otherwise:
" he who kills a man with his sword in fight is a great offender, but he
" is a greater offender who poisons another; for in the one case he, who
" is openly assaulted, may defend himself, and knows his adversary, and
" may endeavour to prevent it; but poisoning may be done so secretly
" that none can defend himself against it, for which cause the offence is
" the more dangerous, because the offender cannot easily be known; and
" of such nature is libelling, it is secret, and robs a man of his good
" name, which ought to be more precious to him than his life, & *diffi-*
" *cillimum est invenire authorem infamatoriæ scripturæ*; and therefore, when
" the offender is known, he ought to be severely punished. Every infa-
" mous libel, *aut est in scriptis, aut sine scriptis*; a scandalous libel *in*
" *scriptis* is, when an epigram, rhime, or other writing is composed or
" published to the scandal or contumely of another. And such libel may
" be published, 1. *verbis aut cantilenis*; as where it is maliciously repeated
" or sung in the presence of others. 2. *Traditione*, when the libel, or any
" copy of it, is delivered over to scandalize the party. *Famosus libellus*
" *sine scriptis* may be, 1, *picturis*, as to paint the party in any shamefull
" and ignominious manner. 2, *signis*, as to fix a gallows, or other re-
" proachful and ignominious signs at the partys door, or elswhere. And
" it was resolved, *Mich.* 43 and 44 *Eliz.* in the *Star-chamber* in *Halli-*
" *woods* case, That if one finds a libel (and would keep himself out of
" danger) if it be composed against a private man, the finder either may
" burn it, or presently deliver it to a magistrate: but if it concern a ma-
" gistrate, or other public person, the finder ought presently to deliver it
" to a magistrate, to the intent that by examination and industry, the
" author may be found out and punished. And libelling and calumnia-
" tion is an offence against the law of God. For Levit. 17. *Non facias*
" *calumniam proximo.* Exod. 22, v. 28. *Principi populi tui non maledices.*

" Eccles.

" Eccles. 10. *In cogitatione tua ne detrahas regi, nec in secreto cubiculi*
" *tui diviti maledices, quia volucres cæli portabunt vocem tuam, & qui*
" *habet pennas annunciabit sententiam.* Psal. 69. 13. *Adversus me loque-*
" *bantur qui sedebant in porta, & in me psallebant qui bibebant vinum.*
" Job. 30. v. 7, and 8. *Filii stultorum & ignobilium, & in terra penitus*
" *non parentes, nunc in eorum canticum versus sum, & factus sum eis in pro-*
" *verbium.* And it was observed that *Job*, who was the mirrour of
" patience, as appears by his words, became *quodammodo* impatient when
" libels were made of him; and therefore it appears of what force they
" are to provoke impatience and contention. And there are certain
" marks by which a libeller may be known; *quia tria sequuntur defama-*
" *torem famosum:* 1, *pravitatis incrementum,* increase of lewdness: 2,
" *bursæ decrementum,* decrease of money, and beggary: 3, *conscientiæ*
" *detrimentum,* shipwrack of conscience."

" John Lambs *case.*"

" Mich. 8. Jacobi."

" *In the Star-Chamber.*"

" *John Lamb,* proctor of the ecclesiastical court, exhibited a bill in
" the Star-chamber against *William Marche, Robert Harrison,* and many
" others of the town of *Northampton,* and against *Shucburgh* and others,
" for publishing two libels. It was resolved, That every one who shall
" be convicted in the said case, either ought to be a contriver of the libel,
" or a procurer of the contriving of it, or a malicious publisher of it,
" knowing it to be a libel; for if one reads a libel, that is no publication
" of it; or if he hears it read, it is no publication of it; for before he
" reads or hears it, he can't know it to be a libel; or if he hears or reads
" it, and laughs at it, it is no publication of it; but, if after he has read
" or heard it, he repeats it, or any part of it in the hearing of others,
" or after that he knows it to be a libel he reads it to others, that is an
" unlawful publication of it; or if he writes a copy of it, and does not
" publish it to others, it is no publication of the libel; for every one
" who

" who fhall be convicted ought to be contriver, procurer or publifher
" of it, knowing it to be a libel.   But it is great evidence that he pub-
" lifhed it, when he, knowing it to be a libel, writes a copy of it; unlefs
" afterwards he can prove that he delivered it to a magiftrate to examine
" it; for then the act fubfequent explains his intention precedent.   *Vide*
" reader, *Bract. lib.* 3. *tract de Corona, cap.* 36, *fo.* 155. *Fiat autem injuria,*
" *cum quis pugno percuffus fuerit, verberatus, vulneratus, feu fuftibus cæfus;*
" *verum etiam cum ei convitium dictum fuerit; vel de eo factum carmen*
" *famofum.*"

Hereupon it may be obferved, 1, that *Coke* was attorney general when
the firft cafe, and chief juftice when the fecond was adjudged.   2, By the
ftat. 3 *Hen.* VII. it was ordained that the chancellor and treafurer, and the
keeper of the kings privy feal, or two of them, calling to them a bifhop
and a temporal lord of the kings moft honorable privy council, and the
two chief juftices of the kings bench and common pleas, or other two
juftices in their abfence, fhould have authority to punifh certain offenders; and by the ftat. 21 *Hen.* VIII. the prefident of the conncil was made
their affociate.   After the making of thefe ftatutes it was held that the
former did not raife a new court; but related wholly to the court of ftar-
chamber; of which lord *Bacon*, in his hiftory of *Henry* the VIIth, after
mentioning the aforefaid ftatute, fays. " This court is compounded of
" good elements, for it confifteth of four kinds of perfons, counfellors,
" pears, prelates, and chief judges.   It difcerneth principally of four
" kinds of caufes, forces, frauds, crimes various of ftellionate, and the
" inchoations or middle acts towards crimes capital or heinous not actually
" committed or perpetrated." Now *ftellionate* is a mere *civil* law term,
denoting all frauds for which there is no particular denomination, and
feveral kinds of fraud are punifhed *criminaliter* by that law under the
name of *ftellionate* that are not liable to any criminal profecution by the
laws of *England*.   3, It does not appear by what members of the court the
refolutions contained in either of thefe cafes were made, judgment being
pronounced according to the majority of voices.   4, It is not improbable
that the bifhop was influenced by the *civil* law, which fo far governed
in his own court, and he might influence others.   Archbifhop *Laud*, who
was frequently lefs referved in declaring his opinion, or his reafons, than
fome of his brethren, when judgement was given againft *Baftwick, Burton,*

and

and *Prynne*, on which occafion he was the chief fpeaker, obferved that the punifhment of libels was in fome cafes capital by the *Imperial* laws, as appeared by the *Code*, l. 9. t. 36, meaning the edict of *Valentinian* and *Valens* aforecited.   5, No precedent, or authority at common law, faving the fingle paffage in *Bracton*, which is evidently taken from *Juftinians* inftitutes, is cited to warrant the refolutions made in thefe cafes; and if thefe judges were influenced by the *civil* law informing them, it cannot reafonably be expected that they fhould exprefsly acknowledge that influence at the time when they refolved that their fellow-fubjects cenfuring their conduct, or that of others, fhould become liable to fuch fevere penalties, as in fome cafes to be difmember'd for it, whereby they feem to have inclined to the feverity of the *Imperial* laws as far as their power would permit, capital offences not being within their cognizance.———And thus having ftated the preceding particulars, I fhall leave the point of influence of the *Imperial* laws upon thefe refolutions, which in feveral refpects fo far refembled them, to the judgment of others.

But thefe two ftar-chamber cafes not only containing, according to lord *Cokes* account of them, a body of laws touching libels, but the fame having been from time to time before and fince the revolution quoted and relied on by the crown lawyers, references made to them, as primary authorities, by fubfequent reporters, and the principal refolutions they contain delivered for law by other authors, one of whom, the author of the treatife intitled " State Law, or the doctrine of Libels difcuffed and exa-" mined," fpeaking of the firft cafe fays, " This cafe contains the beft " fyftem of the doctrine of libels that is to be found, and one would think " is fo full and plain as that all future doubts that could arife in this " learning might be fettled and expounded by it," I fhall endeavour in the next place to give them a proper examination, fo far as relates to my propofition, and thereupon fhall firft confider their authority, and for that end fet forth the origin and abolition of this court, with fome other particulars relative to it.

Sir *Henry Spelman*, in his difcourfe upon the original of the terms, fays, " As for the ftar-chamber, it is in lieu of that which was in ancient time " the counfel-chamber, and *fpecula regni*, the watch-tower of the king-" dom; where the barons and other of the kings counfel ufed to meet

" *ad*

" *ad prospiciendam fovendamque remp.* to discover, prevent, and suppress
" all dangers and enormities occurrent, and to provide for the safety and
" good of the kingdom."

Lord *Bacon*, in his history aforementioned, says, " the authority of
" the star-chamber, which before subsisted by the ancient common laws
" of the realm, was confirmed in certain cases by act of parliament.
" This court is one of the sagest and noblest institutions of this kingdom.
" For in the distribution of courts of ordinary justice (besides the high
" court of parliament) in which distribution the kings bench holdeth
" the pleas of the crown, the common place pleas civil, the exchequer
" pleas concerning the kings revenue, and the chancery the pretorian
" power for mitigating the rigour of law, in case of extremity, by the
" conscience of a good man ; there was nevertheless always reserved a
" high and preeminent power to the kings council, in causes that might
" in example or consequence concern the state of the common wealth ;
" which if they were criminal, the council used to sit in the chamber
" called the star-chamber ; if civil, in the white chamber, or white-hall.
" And as the chancery had the pretorian power for equity ; so the star-
" chamber had the censorian power for offences under the degree of
" capital."

Ld. *Coke*, in his 4th. institute, chap. 5. which treats of, " The hon-
" ourable court of star-chamber, *coram rege & concilio suo* ; of ancient
" time *coram rege in camera*, &c." says, " It is the most honourable court
" (our parliament excepted) that is in the *Christian* world, both in re-
" spect of the judges of the court, and of their honourable proceeding
" according to their just jurisdiction, and the ancient and just orders of
" the court ; for the judges of the same are (as you have heard) the gran-
" dees of the realm, the lord chancellor, the lord treasurer, the lord pre-
" sident of the kings councel, the lord privy seal, all the lords spiritual,
" temporal, and others of the kings most honourable privy councel, and
" the principal judges of the realm, and such other lords of parliament
" as the king shall name.   And they judge upon confession, or deposition
" of witnesses : and the court cannot sit for hearing of causes under the
" nnmber of eight at the least.   And it is truly said, *curia cameræ stellatæ*,
" *si vetustatem spectemus, est antiquissima ; si dignitatem, honoratissima.* This
                                                                                    court,

" court, the right inftitution and ancient orders thereof being obferved,
" doth keep all *England* in quiet."

" Albeit the ftile of the court be *coram rege & concilio*, yet the kings
" councel of that court hear and determine caufes there, and the king in
" judgment of law is always in court."

Rufhworth, in his hiftorical collections [*p*], has given an abftract of
a treatife written by a perfon well acquainted with the proceedings of this
court, wherein, among other things, it is faid that, " without perad-
" venture thofe good laws made in *Edward* IIIds. time, to preferve the
" liberty of the fubject, were chiefly grounded upon the unlimited power
" which this court did then take to itfelf." And afterwards that, " This
" court for the moft part is replenifhed with dukes, marqueffes, earls,
" barons ; alfo with reverend arch-bifhops and prelates, grave councellors
" of ftate, learned judges, fuch a compofition for juftice, religion, and
" government as may be well and truly faid (whilft fo great a prefence
" kept within their bounds) *Mercy and truth were met together.*"

" Their number in the reign of *Henry* VII. and *Henry* VIII. have
" been near forty at one time, and thirty in the reign of *Elizabeth* oft
" times ; but fince much leffened. In king *Charles* time there hath
" been twenty four and twenty fix at a time, as in the cafes of Mr. *Cham-*
" *bers*, Sir *James Bagg*, the bifhop of *Lincoln*, and others."

" Archbifhop *Whitgift* did conftantly in this court maintain the liberty
" of the *free charter*, that none ought to be fined but *falvo contenemento* ;
" he feldom gave any fentence, but therein did mitigate in fomething the
" acrimony of thofe that fpake before him ; but the flavifh punifhment of
" whipping, &c. was not heard to come from the noble fpirits in thofe
" times fitting in that honourable prefence."

" When once this court began to fwell big, and was delighted with
" blood which fprung out of the ears and fhoulders of the punifhed, and
" nothing would fatisfy the revenge of fome clergymen but cropt ears,
" flit nofes, branded faces, whipt backs, gag'd mouths, and withal to be
" thrown into dungeons, and fome to be banifhed not only from their
" native country to remote iflands, but by order of that court to be fepa-

[*p*] Vol. IId.

rated

" rated from wife and children, who were by their order not permitted
" to come near the prifon where their hufbands lay in mifery, then began
" the *Englifh* nation to lay to heart the flavifh condition they were like
" to come unto if this court continued in its greatnefs." Then follow
records touching ancient proceedings in this court, tranfcribed out of
manufcripts which remained there, and among them the following, to
wit,

" *Trin. 8. Eliz. fol.* 138."

" Ordinances for reformation of diforders in printing and felling of
books."

To elucidate this matter I fhall, from the 3d. Inftitute, fet forth the
ftat. 3 *Hen.* VII.

" It is ordained that the chancelour and treafurer of *England,* and the
" keeper of the kings privy feal, or two of them, calling to them a bifhop
" and a temporal lord of the kings moft honourable privy council, and
" the two chief juftices of the kings bench and common pleas for the
" time being, or other two juftices in their abfence, upon bill or infor-
" mation [*q*] put to the faid lord chancelour or any other againft any perfon
" for unlawful maintenance, giving of liveries, figns and tokens, and re-
" tainers by indentures, promifes, oaths, writings or otherwife, imbrace-
" ries of his fubjects, untrue demeaning of fheriffs in making of pannels,
" and other untrue returns by taking of money, by injuries, by great riots,
" and unlawful affemblies, have authority to call before them by writ
" or privy feal the faid mifdoers, and they and other by their difcretion,
" by whom the truth may be known to examine, and fuch as they find
" therein defective, to punifh them after their demerits, after the form
" and effect of ftatutes thereof made, in like manner and form as they
" fhould and ought to be punifhed if they were thereof convict after the
" due order of law."

[*q*] *Quære* whether informations did not originate in this court.

" Lord

" Lord *Coke*, after having treated of the court of ftar-chamber, and
" fet forth this ftatute, from the whole draws fix conclufions, whereof
" the fourth is this."   Fourthly, this Act in one point is introductory of
" a new law, which the former court had not, viz. to examine the de-
" fendant, which being underftood after his anfwer made, to be upon
" oath upon interrogatories, which this ancient court proceeding in cri-
" minal caufes had not, nor could have but by act of parliament, or pre-
" fcription, the want whereof, efpecially in matters of frauds and deceits
" (being like birds clofely hatched in hollow trees) was a mean that truth
" could not be found out; but before the ftatute the anfwer was upon
" oath."

This act exprefsly acknowledges that the perfons who fhould be punifhed by force of it were not to be convicted after the due order of law;
and as the fafety of the fubject requires that they be convicted only according to the due order of law, innocence of the crime being infufficient to
fecure the party accufed when a departure from the due courfe of law
takes place in the proceedings, it may be faid, in my opinion, to have
born teftimony againft itfelf.   Ld. *Coke* takes no notice of this part of the
act, nor that the courfe of judicial proceedings eftablifhed by it was inconfiftent with the Great Charter, which, in the proeme to his commentaries
thereon, he had before obferved had been confirmed, eftablifhed and commanded to be put in execution by thirty two feveral acts of parliament;
but favouring the new law thereby introduced, which gave power to the
judges appointed by the act, according to their conftruction, to examine
the defendant after his anfwer made, upon oath upon interrogatories, at
their difcretion, he affigns a reafon for giving this power, which refpects
all the offences committed to their cognizance, tho' more efpecially frauds,
to wit, that " the want of it was a mean that truth could not be found
" out."   After making this act, the party accufed, inftead of being tried
by his peers, on prefentment or indictment, and convicted upon lawful
evidence, the witneffes appearing perfonally in open court, and giving
their teftimony *viva voce*, fubject to that occafional and free examination
which beft difcovers the truth, was not only liable to be tried by the
judges thus appointed, on a bare information, by the written depofition
of witneffes, made on examination upon interrogatories out of court;
but

but moreover compellable by fine and imprisonment, to give evidence against himself, contrary to the excellent maxim of our constitution, *nemo tenetur seipsum prodere, no man is obliged to betray himself* ; and it appears to me somewhat extraordinary that Sir *Edwᵈ Coke* should thus far approve of this compulsory power, especially considering what himself had before said in his commentary on the 29th chapter of *Magna Charta*, which provides that no freeman shall be condemned but by the lawful judgment of his peers, nor passed upon but by the law of the land, that is, by the due course and process of law ; viz. " Against this ancient and funda-

11. H. VII. cap. 3.

" mental law, and in the face thereof, I find an Act of parliament made,
" that as well justices of assise as justices of peace (without any finding
" or presentment by the verdict of twelve men) upon a bare information
" for the king before them made, should have full power and authority
" by their discretions to hear and determine all offences and contempts
" committed or done by any person or persons against the form, ordinance
" and effect of any statute made and not repealed &c. By colour of which
" act, shaking this fundamental law, it is not credible what horrible op-
" pressions and exactions, to the undoing of infinite numbers of people,
" were committed by Sir *Richard Empson*, and *Edmᵈ Dudley*, being
" justices of the peace, thro' out *England* ; and upon this unjust and
" injurious act (as commony in like cases it falleth out) a new office was
" erected, and they made masters of the kings forfeitures."

1. H. VIII. cap. 6.

" But at the parliament holden in the first year of *Hen.* VIII, this act
" of 11 *H.* VII. is recited, and made void, and repealed, and the reason
" thereof is yielded, for that by force of the said act, it was manifestly
" known, that many sinister and crafty, feigned and forged informations,
" had been pursued against divers of the kings subjects, to their great
" damage, and wrongful vexation : and the ill success hereof, and the
" fearful ends of these two oppressors, should deter others from com-
" mitting the like, and should admonish parliaments, that instead of this
" ordinary and pretious trial *per legem terræ*, they bring not in absolute
" and partial trialls by discretion."—This passage, by the way, is submit-
" ted to the consideration of the promoters of excise laws.

And

And this author, in the firft chapter of his fourth Inftitute, wherein he treats, " of the High Court of Parliament," refuming this fubject, writes as follows,

" There was an act of parliament made in the 11 year of king *Hen.* VII. " which had a fair flattering preamble, pretending to avoid divers mif- " chiefs, which were, 1, To the high difpleafure of Almighty God. 2, " The great let of the common law, and 3, The great let of the wealth " of this land : and the purview of that act tended in the execution con- " trary, *ex diametro*, viz. to the high difpleafure of Almighty God, the " great let, nay the utter fubverfion of the common law, and the great " let of the wealth of this land, as hereafter fhall manifeftly appear. " Which act followeth in thefe words :"

The king our foveraign lord calling to his remembrance that many ftatutes and ordinances be made for the punifhment of riots, unlawful affemblies, reteinders in giving and receiving of liveries, figns and tokens unlawfully, extortions, maintenances, imbracery, exceffive taking of wages contrary to the ftatute of labourers and artificers, the ufe of unlawful games, inordinate apparel, and many other great enormities and offences, which been committed and done daily contrary to the good ftatutes, for many and divers behoveful confiderations feverally made and ordained, to the difpleafure of Almighty God, and the great let of the common law and wealth of this land, notwithftanding that generally by the juftices of the peace in every fhire within this realm in the open feffions is given in charge to enquire of many offences committed contrary to divers of the faid ftatutes and divers enquefts thereupon there ftraitly fworn, and charged before the faid juftices to enquire of the premiffes, and therein to prefent the troth which any letted to be found by imbracery, maintenance, corruption and favour ; by occafion whereof the faid ftatutes be not, nor cannot be put in due execution : For reformation whereof, for fo much that before this time the faid offences, extortions, contempts, and other the premiffes might not, nor as yet may be conveniently punifhed by the due order of the law, except it were firft found and prefented by the ver- dict of twelve men thereto duly fworn, which for the caufes afore re- hearfed will not find nor yet prefent the truth : Wherefore be it by the advice and affent of the lords fpiritual and temporal, and the commons

in

in this prefent parliament affembled, and by authority of the fame enacted, ordained and eftablifhed, that from henceforth as well the juftices of affife in the open feffions to be holden afore them, as the juftices of peace in every county of the faid realm, [a] upon information for the king before them to be made, have full power and authority [b] by their difcretion to hear and determine all offences and contempts committed and done by any perfon or perfons againft the form, ordinance and effect of [c] any ftatute made and not repealed, and that the faid juftices upon the faid information have full power and authority to award and make like procefs againft the faid offenders and every of them, as they fhould or might make againft fuch perfon or perfons as been prefent and indicted before them of trefpafs done contrary to the kings peace, and the faid offender or offenders duly to punifh according to the purport, form and effect of the faid ftatutes. Alfo be it enacted by the faid authority, that the perfon which fhall give the faid information for the king fhall by the difcretion of the juftices content and pay to the faid perfon or perfons againft whom the faid information fhall be fo given his reafonable cofts and damages in that behalf fuftained, if that it be tried or found againft him that fo giveth or maketh any fuch information. Provided always that any fuch information extend not to treafon, murder, or felony, nor to any other offence wherefore any perfon fhall lofe life, or member, nor to lofe by nor upon the fame information any lands, tenements, goods or chattels to the party making the fame information. Provided alfo that the faid informations fhall not extend to any perfon dwelling in any other fhire than there as the faid information fhall be given or made, faving to every perfon and perfons, cities, and towns, all their liberties and franchifes to them and every of them of right belonging and appertaining.

" By pretext of this law *Empfon* and *Dudley* did commit upon the fub-
" ject unfufferable preffures and oppreffions, and therefore this ftatute was
" juftly foon after the deceafe of *Hen.* VII. repealed at the next parlia-
" ment after his deceafe, by the ftat. of 1 *Hen.* VIII. cap. 6.

" A good caveat to parliaments to leave all caufes to be meafured by the
" golden and ftreight met wand of the law, and not to the incertain and
" crooked cord of difcretion."

" It

[a] Upon information without any indictment.
[b] By their difcretion, and not *fecundum legem & confuetudinem Angl.* as all proceedings ought to be.
[c] Obfolete ftatutes andall, and efpecially fuchastime had fo altered from the original caufe of the makingthereof,aseither they could not at all, or very hardly be obferved and kept.

" It is not almoft credible to forefee, when any maxim or fundamental
" law of this realm is altered, (as elfewhere has been obferved) what dan-
" gerous inconveniences do follow; which moft exprefsly appeareth by this
" moft unjuft and ftrange act of 11 *Hen*. VII. for hereby not only *Empfon*
" and *Dudley* themfelves, but fuch juftices of peace (corrupt men) as
" they caufed to be authorized, committed moft grievous and heavy op-
" preffions, and exactions, grinding of the face of the poor fubjects by
" penal laws (be they never fo obfolete or unfit for the time) by information
" only, without any prefentment or trial by jury, being the ancient birth-
" right of the fubject ; but to hear and determine the fame by their dif-
" cretion, inflicting fuch penalty as the ftatutes not repealed impofed.
" Thefe and other like oppreffions and exactions by or by the means of
" *Empfon* and *Dudley*, and their inftruments, brought infinite treafures to
" the kings cofers, whereof the king himfelf in the end with great grief
" and compunction repented, as in [d] another place we have obferved."

[d] In the Chap'. of the court of Wards and Liv eries.

" This ftat. of 11 *Hen*. VII. we have recited, and fhewed the juft incon-
" veniences thereof, to the end that the like fhould never hereafter be
" attempted in any court of parliament. And that others might avoid
" the fearful end of thofe two time-fervers, *Empfon* and *Dudley*. *Qui*
" *eorum veftigiis infiftunt, eorum exitus perhorrefcant*."

Here we have an exprefs declaration made by parliament, that before
the making of this act the offences thereby intended to be punifhed according to the courfe of judicial proceedings introduced by it, could not
be conveniently punifhed by the due order of the law, except it were
firft found and prefented by the verdict of twelve men thereto duly fworn,
as well as the declaration of lord *Coke*, that proceeding by prefentment
and trial by jury are the ancient birth right of the fubject.

Thefe acts of the 3 and 11 of *Hen*. VII. which fo far refemble each
other, were both apparently made in direct repugnance to the great charter, notwithftanding the different treatment given them by Sir *Edw*[d]. *Coke*.
The former indeed remained in force when this great author wrote his
commentaries; but this, I apprehend, will not juftify his favouring fo
far the power thereby given to compel the perfon accufed to give teftimony againft himfelf, refembling herein the proceedings of the holy office
of inquifition ; and the reafon affigned by him for granting this extraordinary

dinary power, to wit, that it is a mean of finding out the truth, is, as we have feen, the fole reafon whereon the ufe of torture is founded by the *civil* law. To all which let us add what is faid by baron *Puffendorf* [r], " that as no man is bound to accufe himfelf in the civil court, or to make " any voluntary confeffion of his crimes, fo it is unjuft in criminal cafes " to put the prifoner to declare his innocence upon oath."

Lord *Cokes* laft conclufion drawn from the ftat. 3 *Hen.* VII. and from what he had faid refpecting the court of ftar-chamber, is, " that the ju- " rifdiction of this court dealeth not with any offence that is not *malum* " *in fe*, againft the common law, or *malum prohibitum*, againft fome " ftatute ;" and yet, in the cafe of *Eaton* againft *Allen*, in his 4th. Report, it is faid that this court could punifh by their abfolute power what was not punifhable by the ordinary courfe of the law.

The abolition of this court, with the reafons for it, will beft appear from the words of the act of parliament paffed in the fixteenth year of the reign of king *Charles* I. entitled, " An act for the regulation of the " privy council, and for taking away the court commonly called the Star- " chamber," to wit :

" Whereas by the great charter, many times confirmed in parliament, " it is enacted, That no freeman fhall be taken or imprifoned, or diffeifed " of his freehold or liberties, or free cuftoms, or be outlawed or exiled, " or otherwife deftroyed, and that the king will not pafs upon him, or " condemn him but by lawful judgment of his peers, or by the law of the " land ; (2.) and by another ftatute made in the fifth year of the reign of " king *Edward* the third, it is enacted, That no man fhall be attached " by any accufation, nor forejudged of life or limb, nor his lands, tene- " ments, goods nor chattels feized into the kings hands againft the form " of the great charter, and the law of the land ; (3) and by another " ftatute made in the five and twentieth year of the reign of the fame " king *Edward* the third, It is accorded, affented, and eftablifhed, That " none fhall be taken by petition or fuggeftion made to the king, or to " his council, unlefs it be by indictment or prefentment of good and " lawful people of the fame neighbourhood where fuch deeds be done, " in due manner, or by procefs made by writ original at the common

[r] Law of Nature and Nations, B. VIII. Ch. III. § 4.

" law,

" law, and that none be put out of his franchife or freehold, unlefs he be
" duly brought in to anfwer, and fore-judged of the fame by the courfe
" of the law; and if any thing be done againft the fame, it fhall be re-
" dreffed and holden for none: (4) And by another ftatute made in the
" eight and twentieth year of the reign of the fame king *Edward* the
" third, it is amongft other things enacted, That no man, of what eftate
" or condition fo ever he be, fhall be put out of his lands or tenements,
" nor taken, nor imprifoned, nor difinherited, without being brought in to
" anfwer by due procefs of law: (5) And by another ftatute made in
" the two and fortieth year of the reign of the faid king *Edward* the
" third, it is enacted, That no man be put to anfwer without prefent-
" ment before juftices, or matter of record, or by due procefs and writ
" original, according to the old law of the land; and if any thing be
" done to the contrary, it fhall be void in law, and holden for error:
" (6) And by another ftatute made in the fix and thirtieth year of the
" fame king *Edward* the third, it is amongft other things enacted, That
" all pleas which fhall be pleaded in any courts before any the kings
" juftices, or in his other places, or before any of his other minifters,
" or in the courts and places of any other lords within the realm, fhall
" be entered and enrolled in Latin: (7) And whereas by the ftatute
" made in the third year of king *Henry* the feventh, power is given to
" the chancellor, the lord treafurer of *England* for the time being, and
" the keeper of the kings privy feal, or two of them, calling unto them
" a bifhop and a temporal lord of the kings moft honourable council, and
" the two chief juftices of the kings bench and common pleas, for the
" time being, or other two juftices in their abfence, to proceed as in that
" act is expreffed, for the punifhment of fome particular offences therein
" mentioned: (8) And by the ftatute made in the one and twentieth
" year of king *Henry* the eighth, the prefident of the council is affociated
" to join with the lord chancellor and other judges in the faid ftatute of
" the third of *Henry* the feventh mentioned; (9) but the faid judges
" have not kept themfelves to the points limited by the faid ftatute, but
" have undertaken to punifh where no law doth warrant, and to make
" decrees for things having no fuch authority, and to inflict heavier
" punifhments than by any law is warranted."

" II. And

" II. And forafmuch as all matters examinable or determinable before
" the faid judges, or in the court commonly called the ftar-chamber, may
" have their proper remedy and redrefs, and their due punifhment and
" correction by the common law of the land, and in the ordinary courfe
" of juftice elfewhere ; (2) and forafmuch as the reafons and motives
" inducing the erection and continuance of that court do now ceafe ; (3)
" and the proceeding, cenfures, and decrees of that court have by expe-
" rience been found to be an intolerable burthen to the fubject, and the
" means to introduce an arbitrary power and government ; (4) and foraf-
" much as the council-table hath of late times affumed unto itfelf a power
" to intermeddle in civil caufes and matters only of private intereft be-
" tween party and party, and have adventured to determine of the eftates
" and liberties of the fubject contrary to the law of the land, and the
" rights and privileges of the fubject, by which great and manifold mif-
" chiefs and inconveniences have arifen and happened, and much incer-
" tainty by means of fuch proceedings have been conceived concerning
" mens rights and eftates, for fettling whereof, and preventing the like
" in time to come,"

" III. Be it ordained and enacted by the authority of this prefent par-
" liament, That the faid court commonly called the Star-chamber, and
" all jurifdiction, power and authority belonging unto or exercifed in the
" fame court, or by any the judges, officers or minifters thereof, be from
" the firft day of Auguft, in the year of our Lord God one thoufand fix
" hundred forty and one, clearly and abfolutely diffolved, taken away and
" determined ; (2) and that from the faid firft day of Auguft, neither the
" lord chancellor, or keeper of the great feal of *England*, the lord trea-
" furer of *England*, the keeper of the kings privy feal, or prefident of
" the council, nor any bifhop, temporal lord, privy counfellor, or judge,
" or juftice whatfoever, fhall have any power or authority to hear, exa-
" mine or determine any matter or thing whatfoever, in the faid court
" commonly called the Star-chamber, or to make, pronounce or deliver
" any judgment, fentence, order or decree, or to do any judicial or mi-
" nifterial act in the faid court : (3) And that all and every act and acts
" of parliament, and all and every article, claufe and fentence in them,
" and every of them, by which any jurifdiction, power or authority is
" given,

" given, limited or appointed unto the said court commonly called the
" Star-chamber, or unto all, or any the judges, officers or ministers
" thereof, or for any proceedings to be had or made in the said court,
" or for any matter or thing to be drawn into question, examined or de-
" termined there, shall for so much as concerneth the said court of Star-
" chamber, and the power and authority thereby given unto it, be from
" the said first day of August repealed and absolutely revoked and made
" void."

" IV. And be it likewise enacted, That the like jurisdiction now used
" and exercised in the court before the president and council in the mar-
" ches of *Wales*; (2) and also in the court before the president and
" council established in the northern parts: (3) And also in the court com-
" monly called the court of the dutchy of *Lancaster*, held before the
" chancellor and council of that court: (4) And also in the court of ex-
" chequer of the county palatine of *Chester*, held before the chamber-
" lain and council of that court; (5) the like jurisdiction being exercised
" there, shall from the said first day of August, one thousand six hun-
" dred forty and one, be also repealed and absolutely revoked and made
" void; any law, prescription, custom or usage, or the said statute made
" in the third year of king *Henry* the seventh, or the statute made the
" one and twentieth of *Henry* the eighth, or any act or acts of parlia-
" ment heretofore had or made, to the contrary thereof in any wise
" notwithstanding: (6) And that from henceforth no court, council
" or place of judicature shall be erected, ordained, constituted or ap-
" pointed within this realm of *England*, or dominion of *Wales*, which
" shall have, use or exercise the same, or the like jurisdiction, as is, or
" hath been used, practiced or exercised in the said court of Star-
" chamber."

The court of star-chamber with all its legal and assumed jurisdiction
power and authority, being thus dissolved, taken away, and determined,
by reason that decrees unwarranted by law, and without authority had
been there made, and that the proceeding, censures and decrees of the
same were so extremely grievous and pernicious in their nature and effects,
with an inhibition to erect for the future any court which should have or
exercise the same or like jurisdiction as had been therein exercised, the
politic

politic framed by this court for the government of the kingdom with
refpect to libels was thereby annuled ; and all fubfequent attempts to enforce the refolutions of this arbitrary court thus abolifhed, as authoritative
rules or laws ftill fubfifting, are, in my apprehenfion, utterly incompatible with this ftatute, and the rights and liberties of the kingdom.   All
hiftory proves that liberty without its proper fecurity becomes the certain victim of power, its native beauty and excellence tempting the ravifher
not to preferve, but to feize and deftroy it, and a little confideration, I
prefume, will convince the intelligent that in limited monarchies to fubject the liberties of the people, and in particular the liberty of the prefs,
wherein the reft are fo nearly concerned, to the difcretionary, that is the
arbitrary, decifions of a court compofed wholly or chiefly of the princes
privy council, is in effect to prepare for their diminution or fuppreffion,
and in time for their total excifion ; and fuch plainly was the nature of
the decrees and refolutions of this court, whofe proceedings were confor-
mable to the order of the *civil* law, rather than of the fundamental laws
of the land ; and what *Buchanan* faid of the judges in his own country
may well be faid of the judges of this court, that " their government
" was evidently tyrannical, their fole decifions being laws."   All courts
do in courfe form fuch rules, decrees and refolutions as are fuitable to their
own nature ; wherefore the refolutions of this arbitrary court, even while
it fubfifted, could not, I conceive, upon the principles of law, be cited
and urged as proper precedents in the conftitutional courts of the kingdom : but the court of ftar-chamber being, for the caufes, and in the
manner, aforefaid utterly abolifhed, that the refolutions of the fame
thereby loft all future force, or, in other words, were thereby abfolutely
refcinded, fo that they could not *in futuro* be cited urged and received as
law under any denomination whatever, appears to me moft manifeft.   A
deadly fountain being covered up, and buried, its ftreams can no longer
pollute the earth, nor a tree plucked up by the roots continue to bear its
poifonous fruit.   Caufes will ever produce their effects, whether their nature and operations be in feafon attended to or not ; and the parliament
having exprefsly declared that the proceeding, cenfures and decrees of
that court had by experience been found to be an intolerable burthen to
the fubject, and the means to introduce an arbitrary power and government

ment, upon the adoption of these proceedings for the rule of our government can we with reason avoid this conclusion, that the same causes will in time produce the same effects?

But altho' it be thus by act of parliament declared that the proceeding, censures and decrees of the court of Star-chamber, collectively considered, were so extremely burthensome to the subjects, and destructive of their liberties, whereupon the foundation of their authority was taken away; yet having lately seen the writings of several authors, who without particularly considering the intent, force or effect of this statute, or the nature of this court, would establish their resolutions respecting libels as good authorities in law at this day, though they scrupple not to censure their decrees in other matters, seeming to proceed as if they thought it was in their power to select the resolutions of this court for preservation or condemnation at their discretion; for which purpose, among other things, it is said that " *The house of commons* were so eager in their zeal to de-
" stroy what they called *a court of inquisition*, that tho' the bill was of
" so great consequence, yet they sent it up to the lords with only once
" reading it, and without its being ever committed, which was a thing
" perhaps never before heard of in parliament;" and for this lord *Clarendon* is cited; intending thereby, without speaking out, to enervate, if possible, the force of the act, and give strength to those resolutions which they favour; in order effectually to oppose these and all such attempts I shall consider this matter more at large.

The most eminent foreign lawyers declare that historical and philosophical knowledge are necessary to juris-prudence; and it is evident that in free states the former is oft times more especially serviceable in forming a right judgment upon questions that relate to the liberty of the subject. Without duely distinguishing times we should be in danger of adopting for the rule of our conduct the determinations of men devoted to the pleasure of princes impatient of those limitations of power which are prescribed by the law of liberty; wherefore I shall proceed to state such historical matters as may give some light on the present occasion.

James, king of *Scotland*, acceded to the crown of *England* with such notions of regal power as were inconsistent with the constitution of this kingdom. There was an essential difference in the nature of the two monarchies;

monarchies; that of *Scotland* being abfolute, and that of *England* limited: but this prince afcended the *Englifh* throne with intent to reduce
the fubjects of this kingdom to the fame meafure of obedience with his
Scotifh fubjects, and, in plain terms, to govern them both according to
his own will. Thefe erroneous notions refpecting the *Englifh* monarchy
were evidently the chief fource of thofe difficulties and calamities in
which his pofterity and the whole kingdom were involved. Foreign as
well as *Englifh* writers have afcribed to this prince thefe arbitrary notions;
but it feems not to have been generally underftood that with refpect to
Scotland he was an abfolute prince, which power fuiting and confirming
his fenfe of the proper ftate of kings, probably augmented his impatience
of the reftraints of power contained in the *Englifh* conftitution, and occafioned his defign of freeing himfelf from them; wherefore I fhall proceed to fhew what power he had in *Scotland*. Sir *George Mackenzie*, in
his " *Jus Regium*, or the juft and folid foundations of monarchy in
" general, and more efpecially of the monarchy of *Scotland*, main-
" tained againft *Buchanan*, *Napthali*, *Dolman*, *Milton*, &c." writes as
follows.

" The next thing that I am to prove in this my firft propofition, is,
" that our king is an abfolute monarch, and has the fupreme power
" within this his kingdom, and this I fhall endeavour to prove, 1. from
" our pofitive law, 2. by feveral reafons deduced from our fundamental laws
" and cuftoms, 3. from the very nature of monarchy itfelf, and the
" opinion of lawyers who write upon that fubject, and who define abfo-
" lute monarchy to be a power that is not limited or reftricted by co-
" active law. *Arnifaus de effentia majeft. cap. 3. num. 4.*"

" By the 25 *act. parl.* 15. *James* VI. [s]. The parliament does acknow-
" ledge *that it cannot be denied but his majefty is a free prince, of a fove-*
" *reign power, having as great liberties and prerogatives, by the laws of*
" *this realm, and privilege of his crown and diadem, as any other king,*
" *prince or potentate whatfoever.* And by the 2 *act. parl.* 18. *James* VI. [t],
" the parliament confenting to his majeftys reftoring of bifhops, declare

[s] holden at *Edingburgh* the 19th day of December 1597.
[t] holden at *Perth* the 9th day of June 1606.

" and

" and acknowledge the absoluteness of our monarchy, in these words.
" *The remeed whereof properly belongs to his majesty, whom the whole estates,*
" *of their bounden duty, with most hearty and faithful affection, humbly*
" *and truly acknowledge to be a sovereign monarch, absolute prince, judge*
" *and governour over all persons, estates and causes, both spiritual and tem-*
" *poral, within his said realm."*

" And by the first act of that same parliament, *The estates and whole*
" *body of this present parliament, acknowledge all with one voluntar, hum-*
" *ble, faithful, united heart, mind and consent his majestys sovereign authority,*
" *princely power, royal prerogative, and privilege of his crown, over all*
" *persons, estates and causes whatsoever within his said kingdom."*

These statutes having in such express terms declared that the *Scotish*
monarchy was absolute, it is evident there is no occasion to cite the arguments of this learned author drawn from other sources to prove it; but
as the safety of the lives, liberties and estates of the subject depends not
only on known certain just and equal laws, but likewise on the integrity,
indifferency, skill and knowledge of those who are to pass in judgment
upon them, the laws in effect being with respect to the parties concerned
what their application makes them; so that unless the state, after enacting
the best laws, makes proper provision for their due execution, by men of
integrity, indifference, ability and fortitude, those laws will become meer
leaden rules, liable to be bent to and fro, as cunning shall devise, and
power dictate, after observing that the *English* constitution was in part
formed by " the kings committing and distributing his whole power of
" judicature to several courts of justice;" [*u*] and providing that the
justices of those courts should do equal law and execution of right to all
the subjects, without having regard to the kings commands, or other
cause [*w*]; in order to shew how this matter stood in *Scotland*, I shall
set forth an act made in the 8th. parliament of the said king *James*, held
at *Edinburgh* on the 22d. day of May, in the year 1584, entitled,

[*u*] *Coles* 4th. Instit. c. 7.   [*w*] 18 Ed. III. Stat. 4. A. D. 1344.

" *Ane*

" *Ane Act confirming the kingis Majesties Royal power over al Estaites and*
" *subjectes within this realme*",

" FORASMEIKLE as sum persones, being lately called befoir the
" kings majestie, and his secreit councel: to answer upon certaine points
" to have bene inquired of them, concerning sum treasonable, seditious,
" and contumelious speaches, uttered by them in pulpit, schooles and
" utherwaies, to the disdaine and reproch of his heines, his progenitours,
" and present councel, contemptouslie declined the judgement of his
" heines, and his said councel in that behalfe, to the evill exempill of
" utheris to do the like, gif timous remeede be not provided. There-
" foir our soveraine lord, and his three estaites assembled in this present
" parliament, ratifies, and apprevis, and perpetually confirmis the royal
" power and authoritie over al estaites, as weil spiritual as temporal,
" within this realme, in the person of the kingis majestie, our soveraine
" lord, his airs and successours, and als statutis and ordanis that his hie-
" nes, his saidis aires and successours, be themselves and their councelles,
" ar, and in time to cum sal be judges competent to al persones his hienes
" subjectes, of quhatsumever estaite, degree, function, or condition that
" ever they be of, spiritual or temporal, in al matters, quharin they, or
" ony of them sal be apprehended, summound, or charged to answer
" to sik thinges as sal be inquired of them be our said soveraine lord and
" his councell. And that nane of them, quhilkis sall happen to be ap-
" prehended, called, or summound, to the effect foirsaid, presume, or
" tak upon hand to decline the judgement of his hienes, his aires and
" successours, or their councel in the premisses, under the paine of
" treason."

And in order to shew how far the liberty of speech and writing touching public affairs was restrained in *Scotland* by laws passed in this kings
reign, and before his accession to the crown of *England,* it may be observed that the same parliament by a subsequent act provided as follows, —— " it is statute and ordained be our soveraine lord, and his three
" estaites, in this present parliament, that nane of his subjectes (of quhat-
" sum-ever function, degree, or qualities) in time cumming sall presume

" or

" or take upon hand privatly, or publickly, in fermones, declamationes,
" or familiar conferences, to utter ony falfe, flanderous, or untrew
" fpeaches, to the difdaine, reproche, and contempt of his majefty,
" his councel and proceedings, or to the difhonour, hurt, or prejudice of his
" hienes, his parents and progenitoures, or to meddle in the affaires of his
" hienes, and his eftaite prefent, by-gane, and in time cumming, under
" the paines conteined in the acts of parliament againft makers and tellers
" of leefinges [x] : certifying them that fhall be tryed contravenors their-
" of, or that hearis fik flanderous fpeaches, and reportes not the fame with
" diligence, the faid paine fal be execute againft them, with all rigour, in
" exemple of utheris. Attoure, becaufe it is underftand to his hienes
" and to his three eftaites, that the buikes of the chronicle, and *De jure*
" *regni apud Scotos,* made be umquhile maifter GEORGE BUCHANNANE,
" and imprinted fenfine, conteinis findrie offenfive matters worthie to
" be deleete : IT IS THEIRFORE ftatute and ordaned, that the havers
" of the faidis twa volumes in their handes, in bring, and deliver the
" fame to my lord fecretare, or his deputes, within fourtie dayes after
" the publication hereof, to the effect that the faidis volumes may bee
" perufed, and purged of the offenfive and extraordinarie matters fpe-
" cified therein, not meete to remaine as recordes of truth to the
" pofteritie ; under the paine of twa hundreth pundes, of everie perfon
" failzieng heirin. And quhair ony ar not refponfall to pay the faid
" fumme, to be punifhed in their perfones, at OUR SOVERAINE LORDIS
" will. And to the effect that this ordinance may cum to the knaw-
" ledge of all, OUR SOVERAINE LORDIS lieges ordanis publication to
" be maid theirof at the mercat-croce of the head burrowes of the fhires,
" and utheris places needfull, That nane pretend ignorance theirof :
" And the penaltie conteined theirin to be executed with al rigour againft
" the havers of the faidis buikes, the faid fpace of fourty dayes being
" by-paft, after the publication and proclamation of the faid act in every
" fhire, as faidis."

Notwithftanding this cenfure of thefe writings of the celebrated *Bu-*
chanan, another author of great abilities, *Le Clerc,* in his *Bibliothe-*

[x] See the act next cited.

" *que*

que Choiſie, obſerves, " That if *James* VI. had made a right improve-
" ment of his tutor *Buchanans* lectures, he wou'd not have had ſuch
" unhappy diſputes with his parliaments; and if his ſon had been well
" read in *Buchanans* works, and enter'd into his ſentiments, he wou'd
" not have left his head upon a ſcaffold : And his grandſon perhaps,
" who was of his own name, if he had been trained up in the ſame
" notions, wou'd have dyed in peace upon the throne. If they had
" been all perſuaded that they were the protectors, and not the maſters,
" of the laws of their kingdom they wou'd undoubtedly have lived hap-
" pily. If in monarchical ſtates princes were *republicans,* their ſubjects
" wou'd become all *royaliſts,* by reaſon of the confidence they wou'd
" repoſe in their kings. Princes never have more authority than when
" they think, and ſeem fully convinced, that they have no right to
" augment ſuch authority *ad infinitum;* and the people are never
" more obedient than when they are induced by the moderation of
" their princes."

By the 2d. parliament of king *James* Iſt. holden at *Perth* the 12th. day
of March 1424, an act was made in the following words.

" ITEM. It is ordaned be the king and the haill parliament, that
" all leeſing-makers and tellers of them, quhilk may ingender diſcorde
" betwixt the king and his people, quhair ever they may be gotten,
" ſall be challenged be them that power hes, and tine life and gudes
" to the king."

And by the 10th. parliament of king *James* VIth, holden at LIN-
LITHGOW the 10th. day of Decr. 1585, another act was made, entitled,

" *Authours of ſlanderous ſpeaches, or writts, ſuld be puniſhed to the death.*"

" IT IS ſtatute and ordaned, be our SOVERAINE LORD, and three
eſtaites, that all his hienes ſubjectes content themſelves in quietneſs and
dewtifull obedience to his hienes and his authoritie. And that nane of
them preſume, or take upon hand publicklie to declame, or privatly to
ſpeak or write ony purpoſe of reproch, or ſlander of his majeſties perſone,
eſtaite, or governement : Or to deprave his lawes and actes of parliament,

ment, or mifconftrue his proceedinges, quhairby only miflyking may be mooved betwixt his hienes and his nobilitie, and loving fubjectes in time cumming, under the paine of death : Certifieng them that does the contrare, they fal be repute as feditious and wicked inftrumentes, enemies to his hienes and the commoun-weill of this realme. And the faid paine of death fal be execute upon them, with all rigour, in exemple of utheris."

From the preceding acts it appears that king *James* had an abfolute dominion over the kingdom of *Scotland*, with the affent, declaration and confirmation of the reprefentatives of it, accompanied with the moft rigorous laws, reftraining, or rather inhibiting, the ufe of fpeech and writing refpecting himfelf, his family and government ; for their prohibitory terms were fo general, vague and indefinite, that, in my opinion, they left no fafety for the people but in painful filence, relative to thofe fubjects whereon man by his nature is fo much enclined to fpeak his fentiments, efpecially confidering to whofe judgement every fuppofed offender was fubjected. The judicious *Hooker*, in the 10th. fection of his firft book of the Laws of Ecclefiaftical Polity, wherein he confidereth how reafon doth lead men unto the making of human laws, whereby politic focieties are governed, obferves that, " Between men and beafts " there is no poffibility of fociable communion, becaufe the welfpring " of that communion is a natural delight which man hath to transfufe " from himfelf into others, and to receive from others into himfelf, " efpecially thofe things wherein the excellency of his kind doth moft " confift. The chiefeft inftrument of humane communion therefore is " fpeech, becaufe thereby we impart mutually one to another the " conceits of our reafonable underftanding." And government being inftituted for the common good of the fociety its continuance ought certainly to be fuitable to that inftitution ; and every member having an intereft in this continuance, whereon the prefervation of all that is dear to him does depend, it is fo natural for them, in their private or familiar conferences at leaft, to fpeak their minds concerning its adminiftration, and it was fo extremely difficult, if not impoffible, in fuch difcourfes to avoid every thing which might be deemed mifconftruction of this princes proceedings, that it appears to me an excefs of cruelty to fubject them

therefore

therefore to tortures and death: And this sovereign monarch, absolute prince, judge and governour being fallible, thro' his failings particular persons might suffer great hardships: and the minds of many are so formed that their complaints do as naturally ensue on the sense of their sufferings as the shadow follows the substance. *Arnobius*, had he lived in these times, and been acquainted with these laws, might with great reason have said that the *Scots* subjected to the loss of life those who muttered any thing amiss of their king, the representatives of the kingdom having concurred with him in making these severe laws; whereas the *Romans* suffered under laws made, wrested or extended beyond their original intention, by the emperours alone, or thro' the exercise of their open tyranny, without the least regard to any law right or justice, divine or human. And *Gronovius* might have said that the despotic power of king *James* was surrounded with such awful silence as no *Roman* tyrant ever by law enjoyed. For my own part, I am unable to reconcile these *Scotch* laws with the dignity, equity, freedom, innate disposition, or fallibility of human nature, or to conceive their intent force and effect to be less than this, that the subjects being reduced to a state of absolute obedience should so comport themselves as if they esteemed this prince with all his failings infallible, his parents with their misconduct faultless, and his forefathers with all their errors blameless.

Aristotle [y] observes that a king governs willing subjects, according to law; but a tyrant the unwilling; and *Buchanan*, after citing him, says that " a kingdom is the government of a freeman among freemen, " tyranny the government of a master over slaves;" and, without undertaking the defence of his facts or positions, it may be said that he wrote with intent to shew that the kingdom of *Scotland* never was, nor ought to be, held under absolute subjection. On the contrary Sir *George Mackenzie*, who cites no positive law prior to the preceding to prove that the *Scotish* monarchy was absolute, says that the acts by him cited conferred no new right on the king, but only acknowledge what was his right and prerogative from the beginning; whereas this might be a politic method of obtaining such powers as had no prior existence. His arguments

[y] Politic. lib. iii. c. 14.

drawn

drawn from other fources than the pofitive law appear to me inconclufive; but it is unneceffary on the prefent occafion to enter into the merits of this queftion. In cafe king *James* was not an abfolute monarch by the conftitution of the kingdom, but was made fo by ftatutes obtained from parliaments by the too great influence of their monarch, and the too great pufillanimity of parliaments, who could not refign the rights and privileges of the people, fince they had no warrant from them for that effect, as fome fuggefted, this I conceive would rather augment than leffen the hopes of king *James* to obtain and eftablifh the like abfolute power in *England*.

Notwithftanding the notoriety of this princes defigns upon the *Englifh* liberties, continued through the courfe of his reign, I fhall for the illuftration thereof fet forth fome part of his conduct at the beginning of it. On the 3d. of May 1603 he arrived at *Theobalds*, where he made three *Scotch* peers, and Sir *James Elphingftone*, his *Scotch* fecretary, mem- Rymeri
Fœd: bers of his council; and on the 19th. at *Greenwich* he iffued a procla- mation upon the union of the kingdoms of *England* and *Scotland*, wherein, after declaring that he would with the advice of the ftates and parliaments of both kingdoms make the fame perfected, in the mean time, til the faid union fhould be eftablifhed, his majefty did thereby repute hold and efteem, and command all his heighnefs fubjects to repute hold and efteem, both the two realmes as prefently united, and as one realme and kingdom, and the fubjects of both the realmes as one peo- ple, brethren, and members of one body. This immediate union or incorporation of the two kingdoms was apparently an act fuitable to an abfolute fovereignty over both. And there having been a great refort of perfons to fee the king on his arrival, by his proclamation of the 23d. of June, for the reafons therein mentioned, he iffued the following order, Idem. " We will and command all gentlemen and others, as well fuch as have " any kind of charge in the counties of their ordinary habitation, as " of other fort, that yf they have not fome fpeciall caufe of attend- " ance at our court for our fervice, or for fome neceffary caufe concerning " their own eftate, whereof they may inform our privie counfell, they " fhall, ymediatly after the end of this terme, depart our faid cittie of " London; and the fuburbs thereof, and return to their feveral habita-
" tions

" tions in the counties of their abode, untill the time of our coronation
" be come, at what tyme we fhall not mislike to have them retourne
" untill that folempnitie be paffed."

" And bicaufe we perceave that heretofore there hath been a great ne-
" glect in obeying proclamations publifhed upon juft caufes, we do ad-
" monifh all thofe whom this proclamation concerneth, to be fo warie
" as we have not juft caufe to make them an example of contempt, which
" we muft and will do, yf, after the term ended, we fhall fynde anye
" makeinge ftay here contrarie to this direction." And by his proclamation of the 8th of July, for the concord of the *Englifh* and *Scots*,
after declaring that in his *Englifh* fubjects, from the higheft to the
loweft, he had obferved great love, and general obedience to him and
his commandments, he faid that feeing it had pleafed Almighty God
to call him to the *fupreme* power over both [kingdoms] he was pur-
pofed to be an univerfal and equal fovereign to them both. By his
proclamation of the 11th of January, iffued for calling a parliament,
he affumed the power of regulating the elections of the members to be
chofen at his difcretion, and of enforcing his regulations by penal fanctions, fubjecting the cities and boroughs not obferving them to fines,
and to the forfeiture of their liberties; concluding with thefe words,
" and if any perfon take upon him the place of a knight, citizen, or bur-
" geffe, not being duely elected, retorned and fworne, according to the
" lawes and ftatutes in that behalfe provided, and according to the
" purport effect and true meaning of this oure proclamation ; then every
" perfon, foe offending, to be fyned and imprifoned for the fame";
thereby putting his proclamation upon an equal foot with the laws and
ftatutes of the kingdom in points of the greateft importance. In this
proclamation his majefty boafts of his long experience of kingly government, and what fort of government he had experienced has been already
fhewn. According to *Rapin*, " immediately after the opening of the
" parliament, the commons examining, according to cuftom, the con-
" tefted elections, there was a debate in the houfe about the return of
" Sir *Francis Goodwin*, and Sir *John Fortefcue*, for knight of the fhire
" for the county of *Bucks*, and upon a full hearing Sir *Francis* was de-
" clared duly elected. Three days after, the lords fent a meffage to the
commons,

Rymeri Fœd.

Idem.

March, 23d.

" commons, that there might be a conference about *Goodwins* election.
" The commons, furprized at fo extraordinary a meffage, anfwered, they
" did not think themfelves obliged to give an account of their proceed-
" ings, and therefore could not grant the conference required. The
" lords replied, the king having been acquainted with what had paffed
" in *Goodwins* cafe, thought himfelf engaged in honour to have the affair
" debated again, and had ordered them to confer with the commons
" upon it. Whereupon the commons, by their fpeaker, gave their reafons
" to the king why they could not admit of this innovation. But all they
" could obtain was, that, inftead of a conference with the lords, the
" king commanded them to confer with the judges. This pleafed them
" no more than the other. They fet down their reafons in writing, and de-
" livered them at the council chamber, to defire their lordfhips to inter-
" cede for them to the king, not to violate their privileges. The anfwer
" was, the king abfolutely commanded them to have a conference with
" the judges. The commons were extremely furprized at fo abfolute an
" order. Mean while, fearing to be accufed of too eafily engaging in
" a quarrel with the king, they thought it more proper to yield than
" ftand out, fully bent however to adhere to what had been determined
" in the cafe of the contefted election. Certainly the king had engaged
" in a very nice affair, and probably would not have come off with
" honour, had he not been difengaged by *Goodwins* moderation. Sir
" *Francis* chufing to forfeit his right rather than occafion a quarrel be-
" tween the king and the commons, defired the houfe to order the
" county of *Bucks* to elect another knight in his ftead. The king and
" commons equally accepted of this expedient, which prevented them
" from coming to extremities; but the king found from hence that no
" great account was made of the proclamation upon calling the parlia-
" ment, whereby he meant to be mafter of the elections."

On the 17th of October, in the 2d year of his reign, his majefty, by
his letters patent, impofed a duty of fix fhillings and eight-pence on every
pound weight of tobacco which after the 26th day of that month fhould be
imported into the kingdom by any *Englifh* merchants, or ftrangers, or other
perfons, over and above the former cuftom of two pence upon the pound
weight; and thereby provided, that the officers of his cuftoms fhould
thereafter

Rymeri
Fœd.

thereafter fuffer no entries to be made of any tobacco at any time to be imported, before the faid cuftom and impofition fhould be paid, or compofition made for the fame with thofe officers, under the penalties contained in thefe words, " upon payne that if any merchaunte Englifh or " ftraunger, or other whatfoever, fhall prefume to bringe in anye of the " faide *tabacco*, before fuche paymente and fatisfactione firfte made, " That then he fhall not onlie forfeite the faide *tabacco* ; but alfoe fhall " undergoe fuch furthere penalties and corporall punifhmente as the " qualitie of fuche foe highe a contempte againft our royall and ex- " preffe commaundement in this mannere publifhed fhall deferve." And on the 3d of November following his Majefty, by his letters patent, impofed a duty of five fhillings and fixpence on every hundred weight of currans imported. Thefe letters patent are not contained in *Rymers* collections ; but by the firft article of impeachment againft lord chief baron *Davenport*, made in July 1641, it is declared that in Michaelmas term, in the fourth year of the reign of king *Charles*, his majefties then attorney general exhibited an information by *Englifh* bill in the exchequer againft *Samuel Vaffall*, merchant, fetting forth " that king *James*, by his " letters patent dated 3^{tio} *Nov^s.* in the fecond year of his reign, did " command the faid impofition of five fhillings and fix pence upon " every hundred weight of currans fhould be demanded and received ; " and that his majeftie [that then was], by his letters patent, dated the " fix and twentieth day of July, in the fecond year of his reign, did by " advice of his privy-conncil, declare his will and pleafure to be, That " fubfidies ,cuftoms and impoft fhould be levied in fuch manner as they " were in the time of king *James*, and the fame, and the farms thereof " to continue until it might receive a fettling by parliament, and com- " manding the levying and receiving the fame accordingly [*y*]." And by another proclamation, of the 20th of October preceding, for the union of the two kingdoms, his majefty, after faying many things, expreffed himfelf thus in relation to it, " whereof many particularities " depending upon the determination of the ftates and parliamentes of " bothe realms, we leave them there to be difcuffed, according to the " commiffions graunted by the feveral actes of bothe parliamentes, and

[*y*] *Rufhworths* Collections, vol. 4th. p. 334.

" fome

" some other things resting in our own Imperial power as the head of
" both : We are purposed, towards the buildinge of this excellent worke,
" to do by Oureself that which justlie and safelie We may by our *absolute*
" power doe; and for a first stone of this worke, whereupon the rest
" may be laid, seeing there is undoubtedlie but one head to both people,
" which is Oureself, and that unfainedlie we have but one hart and
" mynd to communicate equally to both states, as lynes issuing from one
" center, our justice, our favors, and whatsoever else dependeth upon the
" unitie of our *supreme* power over bothe." After which his majesty
thereby assumed the stile of " King of Great Britain, France and Ireland,
" Defender of the Faith, &c."

Sir *George Mackenzie* supposes that the *Scots* and *English* became *con-vassalli*, the fellow-vassalls of king *James* on his accession to the crown
of *England*; and this prince intending to be the absolute lord over both,
in order to reduce the *English* to this state of obedience, the chief instruments he made use of were his privy council, the court of star-chamber,
his judges and lawyers, the two first being composed of the same persons,
and all holding their places at his pleasure, who expected their compliance with it. The king in his first speech to his parliament expressed
some regard for his *Roman* catholick subjects; but the puritans, he said,
were a " sect unable to be suffered in any well-governed common wealth."
And on the 13th of February following, all the judges being by the kings
command assembled, with many of the nobility, including the great
officers of state, in the star-chamber, to give their opinions touching the
legality of the deprivation of the puritan ministers, and of the petition
of the puritans, after this business was over, many of the lords declared
that some of the puritans had raised a false rumour of the king, that he
intended to grant a toleration to the papists, which offence the judges
held punishable by grievous fine, by the rules of the common law in the
kings bench, or by the king and his council, or, since the stat. of
3 *Hen.* VII. in the star-chamber.

The court of star-chamber in the begining of this reign, by condemn-
ing the parties accused for light offences in exorbitant fines to the kings
use, was become a terrour even to the Great; and by their proceeding
from time to time without just regard to the nature of offences, and of
the

the evidence adduced to prove them, they continued a grievance and terrour, until the amplitude and multiplicity of their oppreſſions cauſed the diſſolution of this court, the neceſſity whereof may be farther evinced from lord *Clarendon*. An unconſtitutional and oppreſſive court ſubſiſting in the North, in order to its abolition, being the manager for the commons of a conference with the lords, held on the 22d of April 1641, he began his ſpeech thus. " I am commanded by the knights, citizens " and burgeſſes of the houſe of commons, to preſent to your lordſhips " a great and crying grievance ; which though it be complained of in " the preſent preſſures but by the northern parts, yet by the logic and " conſequence of it it is the grievance of the whole kingdom. The " court of the preſident and council of the North ; or, as it is more " uſually called, the court of *York* ; which by the ſpirit and ambition of " the miniſters truſted there, or by the natural inclination of courts to " enlarge their own power and juriſdiction, hath ſo prodigiouſly broken " down the banks of the firſt channels in which it ran, hath almoſt " overwhelmed that country under the ſea of arbitrary power, and in- " volved the people in a labyrinth of diſtemper, oppreſſion and poverty." And after giving an account of the erection of this court, 31 *Hen.* VIII. by commiſſion, which was no other than a commiſſion of *oyer* and *terminer*, only that it had a clauſe at the end of it for the hearing of all cauſes real and perſonal. *Quando ambæ partes, vel altera pars, ſic gravata paupertate fuerit, quod commodè jus ſuum ſecundum legem regni noſtri aliter perſequi non poſſit.* Which he ſuppoſed to be illegal, adding that whether they exerciſed that part of the commiſſion at all, or ſo ſparingly that poor people found eaſe and benefit by it, he knew not ; but at that time he found no complaint againſt it. He then ſaid, that, " till the coming " in of king *James*, the commiſſion continued ſtill the ſame, and that " in the firſt year of his reign to the lord *Sheffield* varied no otherwiſe " from the former ; ſave only it had reference to inſtructions which " ſhould be ſent, though whether any were ſent or no is uncertain, for " we can find none. In June, in the 7th year of the reign of king " *James*, a new commiſſion was granted to the ſame man (the lord " *Sheffield)* very differing from all that went before, it being left out, " that they ſhould enquire, *per ſacramentum bonorum & legalium hominum,*

" and

" and to hear and determine *secundum leges Angliæ*; relation being had
" only to the instructions, which were the first instructions we can find
" were sent thither;" and after coming to the instructions and com-
missions under which that part of the kingdom then groaned and lan-
guished, among other things, he said, " I shall not trouble your lord-
" ships with the ninth instruction, though it be but short, which intro-
" duceth that *miseram servitutem, ubi jus est vagum & incognitum,* by re-
" quiring an obedience to such ordinances and determinations as be or
" shall be made by the council table, or high commission court : a griev-
" ance, my lords, howsoever *consuetudo & peccantum claritas nobilitaverit*
" *hanc culpam,* of so transcendent a nature, that your lordships noble justice
" will provide a remedy for it with no less care than you would rescue
" the life and blood of the commonwealth." He observed that the
thirtieth instruction erected such an empire, such a dominion, as should
be liable to no contrary, afterwards saying thus. " What hath the good
" northern people done, that they only must be disfranchised of all their
" privileges by *Magna Charta,* and the Petition of Right ? For to what
" purpose serve these statutes if they may be fined and imprisoned with-
" out law, according to the discretion of the commissioners ?" And in the
subsequent part of his speech he uses these words. " Your lordships
" remember the directions I mentioned of *Magna Charta,* That all pro-
" ceedings shall be *per legale judicium parium, & per legem terræ*; now
" these jurisdictions tell you you shall proceed according to your dis-
" cretion; that is, you shall do what you please; only that we may not
" suspect this discretion will be gentler and kinder to us than the law,
" special provision is made, no fine, no punishment shall be less than
" by the law is appointed, by no means, but as much greater as your
" discretion shall think fit : And indeed in this improvement we find
" arbitrary courts are very pregnant : If the law require my good be-
" haviour, this discretion makes me close prisoner; if the law sets me
" upon the pillory, this discretion appoints me to leave my ears there."
How far what is here said may well be applied to the court of star-
chamber is obvious. And his lordship, in his history of the Rebellion,
after taking notice that projects of all kinds, many ridiculous, many scandalous, all very grievous, were set on foot; and mentioning ship-money

with others, writes thus. " For the better fupport of thefe extraordi-
" nary ways, and to protect the agents and inftruments who muft be
" employed in them, and to difcountenance and fupprefs all bold en-
" quiries and oppofers, the council-table, and ftar-chamber enlarge their
" jurifdictions to a vaft extent, holding (as *Thucydides* faid of the *Athe-*
" *nians*) for honourable that which pleafed, and for juft that which
" profited ; and being the fame perfons in feveral rooms, grew both
" courts of law to determine right, and courts of revenue to bring money
" into the treafury ; the council-table by proclamations enjoyning to the
" people what was not enjoyned by the law, and prohibiting that which
" was not prohibited ; and the ftar-chamber cenfuring the breach and
" difobedience to thofe proclamations by very great fines, and imprifon-
" ment ; fo that any difrefpect to any acts of ftate, or to the perfons of
" ftates-men, was in no time more penal, and thofe foundations of right
" by which men valued their fecurity, to the apprehenfion and under-
" ftanding of wife men, never more in danger to be deftroyed."

Could *Selden*, *Milton*, or colonel *Titus* in ftronger terms defcribe the
defpotic domination exercifed over the people of *England*, and enforced
by the court of ftar-chamber, or can it now be faid that this the chief
engine of lawlefs dominion was not become fit for excifion, or that its
doctrines, decrees, and proceedings were worthy of perpetual imitation,
force, and obligation ?

With refpect to the proceeding of the houfe of commons, which concluded in paffing a bill for the diffolution of the court of ftar-chamber,
it may be obferved that on the 1ft of Decr. 1640 the petition of *Richard*
Chambers of *London*, merchant, delivered in a former parliament, was
read, complaining of his fentence in the ftar-chamber, 4 and 5 *Car.* and
of the proceedings of the barons of the exchequer in relation to his
goods feized at the cuftom-houfe. After this petition was read, Mr.
Vaffall, a member of the houfe, delivered his grievances by word of
mouth, much of the fame nature with thofe of Mr. *Chambers* as to
the court of exchequer ; whereupon a committee was appointed to confider this petition and complaint, with power to fend for parties, witneffes, papers, records, or any thing elfe that might conduce to this
bufinefs, and to meet in the exchequer-chamber. On the fame day the
                                                                        feveral

several petitions of *William Prynn*, formerly a barrister at law, late exile and close prisoner in the isle of *Jersey*, of *Henry Burton* [formerly minister of the parish church of St. *Mathew* Fridayſtreet] late exile and close prisoner in castle *Cornet* in the isle of *Garnsey*, and of *John Baſt-wick*, doctor in physic, lately retained close prisoner and exile in the isle of *Scilly*, were presented and read. Mr. *Prynn* complained of certain proceedings against him in the court of star-chamber, for writing his *Histrio-mastix*, for which he was fined *£.* 5000 to his majesty, expelled the university of *Oxford*, and *Lincolns-inn*; degraded, put from his profession of the law, set in the pillory in the palace-yard, *Westminster*, where he lost one of his ears, and three days after on the pillory in *Cheap-side*, where he lost the other ear, his books which had been licenced being there publickly burned before his face by the hang-man, and was adjudged after all this to remain a prisoner during his life [a]; and complained that after the said censure, to defame and injure him the more, he was charged wrongfully in the decree, as censured for perjury, though not taxed for it by the court; and after mentioning the illegal taking away of his books between his sufferings in the pillory, which had been twice surveyed, and restored to him by order of the lords, by warrant from the high commission, signed by archbishop *Laud* and others, complained that afterwards, by an indirect order procured out of the said court of star-chamber, sent to the tower to be executed, he was shut up close prisoner, and Dr. *Reeves* sent thither to search for a pamphlet which the archbishop would have father'd upon him; and that about three years and half before presenting this petition, during his imprisonment, by means of the said archbishop, a new information was exhibited in the said court against him and others, with certain books annexed, opposing the hierarchy, and censuring the proceedings of the bishops, the high-commission and ecclesiastical courts in various respects; and that although no witness was produced to prove him either author or disperser of any of the said books; yet by denying him liberty to draw up his own answer,

[a] The tryal of Mr. *Prynn* and others began the 7th of Feb. 1633. It does not appear from the State tryals when this sentence was pronounced; but it was executed on the 7th and 10th of May following.

when

when his counfel affigned refufed to do it, by clofe imprifoning himfelf and his fervant, by debaring him pen, ink and paper whereby to anfwer or inftruct his counfel, fearching his chamber, and taking away part of his anfwer there found; denying him accefs to his counfel, and conference with his co-defendants, even at counfel; threatening one of his counfel fent by the lord keeper to the tower to draw up his anfwer, and commanding him not to fign it when engroffed, and by refufing to accept his anfwer figned by himfelf, and his other counfel, though tendered at the office, and in open court at the hearing, the faid information was taken *pro confeffo*, and he was thereupon fined £. 5000 to his majefty, pillored, ftigmatized on both cheeks, and the remainder of his ears cut off, to the hazard of his hearing and life, and adjudged to perpetual clofe imprifonment in the goal of *Carnarvan* caftle, which he calls a nafty dog-hole; and that after the execution of this fentence he applied to the archbifhop, defiring him to releafe or bail his fervant, who was detained clofe prifoner ten weeks in a meffengers hands, and often examined and follicited by promifes and threats caufelefsly to accufe the petitioner, againft whom they wanted evidence, fo that he might attend him during his fores, which the archbifhop utterly refufed, faying that he intended to proceed againft him in the high commiffion court, where he had ever fince vexed, cenfured and banded him from prifon to prifon, only for refufing to accufe and betray the petitioner; and alfo that in addition to this laft heavy fentence he was by an order in the faid court inhibited the ufe of pen, ink and paper, and all books, except the bible, common-prayer, and fome books of devotion; and after mentioning his removal from the tower to *Carnarvan*, before his wounds were perfectly cured, and the citation of his friends who vifited him in his paffage, to appear before the lords of the privy-council, and their profecution therefore in the high commiffion court, though his conductors had no order to reftrain any perfon from reforting to him; and after mentioning fundry grievances fuffered by himfelf, and his friends on his account, by various ecclefiaftical proceedings, he complained that after continuing ten weeks clofe prifoner in *Carnarvan*, he was by a warrant from the lords of the council ordered to be tranfported as an exile into one of the caftles in the ifle of *Jerfey*, permitting his conductors only to fpeak with him in his paffage;

whereupon

whereupon he was embarked in a leaky veffel, and after a very tedious and dangerous paffage in the winter feafon arriving at the faid ifland he was made clofe prifoner in *Mount Orguile* caftle, where the lieutenant governor by another extrajudicial order was commanded to confine him clofe in a chamber, to fuffer none but his keepers to fpeak with him, to intercept all letters to him, to permit him neither pen, ink, nor paper, either to write to his friends for neceffaries, or to petition for relief, and to allow him only the books aforementioned, without giving any order for his dyet; fo that he had certainly perifhed, in his almoft three years clofe imprifonment, if not fuftained by the noble charity of his keepers: Whereupon he prayed the honourable houfe to take his tragical grievances of near eight years continuance, of new and dangerous example, into their juft confideration, that they might not become precedents to the prejudice of pofterity, and to grant him the proper orders requifite for the effectual fupport of his petition, with fuch relief as the juftice of his caufe fhould merit.

Mr. *Burton* fet forth that, having on the 5th of November 1636 preached two fermons in his own parifh church, he was thereupon fummoned to appear before Dr. *Duck,* one of the commiffioners for caufes ecclefiaftical, at *Chefwick,* and having ftated the proceedings before that judge, with his appeal to the king, he complained that notwithftanding his appeal, entered in writing by Dr. *Ducks* direction, a fpecial high commiffion court fhortly after called at *London,* illegally fufpended him in his abfence, by means whereof, and of the faid commiffioners threats, he kept his houfe til a ferjeant at arms, with divers purfevants and other armed officers, affifted by the fheriff of *London,* at eleven of the clock at night forcibly brake into his houfe, took out of his ftudy fuch books as they pleafed, and carried him to prifon, and the next day, the 2d of February, by a pretended order from the lords of the council, he was conveyed to the fleet, and there clofely imprifoned, during which imprifonment he was, by information exhibited in the court of ftar-chamber, charged, *inter alia,* with publifhing a book containing *An Apology for an appeal,* with his two fermons entitled *God and the King.* He then fet forth the making of his anfwer with the advice of his counfel, who figned it, the admiffion of it, and the fubfequent reference thereof to

the

the two chief Juftices, who expunged the whole as impertinent and fcandalous, fave only the *Not Guilty*, with other proceedings confufedly ftated, as they ftand in *Rufhworth*; after which he complained that the information being taken *pro confeffo* the court cenfured him in a fine of £ 5000 to the king, to be deprived of his benefice, degraded from his minifterial function and degrees in the univerfity, and ordered to be fet on the pillory, both his ears to be cut off, confined to perpetual clofe imprifonment in *Lancafter* caftle, debarred the accefs of his wife, or any other but his keeper, and denied the ufe of pen, ink and paper, all which, except the fine, was executed accordingly; and that after twelve weeks clofe imprifonment in the common goal of that caftle, he was, to the hazard of his health and life, by an extrajudicial order, tranfported in the winter feafon to the caftle of *Guernfey*, where he remained near three years, and his wife prohibited on pain of imprifonment, to fet her foot on the ifland, contrary to the laws of God and the liberties of the kingdom. Whereupon he prayed the honourable houfe to take his caufe into confideration, to affign him counfel, and grant him an order for the copies requifite for the maintenance of it.

Dr. *Baftwick*, after reprefenting that he had about fix years before fet out a book in Latin, called *Elenchus religionis papifticæ*, with an addition called *Flagellum Pontificis, & epifcoporum Latialium*, wherein, to prevent the mifinterpretation of his good intentions, he had fully declared in his epiftle to the reader, that he meant nothing againft fuch bifhops as acknowledged their authority from kings and emperours; yet becaufe, the better to fhew the papal ufurpation over other princes, he had by way of argument maintained, like other orthodox writers on that fubject, a parity of the faid bifhop of *Rome* and all other bifhops and prefbyters, denying his and their fupremacy over other minifters to be by divine inftitution, complained that a purfivant did by authority from the high commiffion court thereupon, in his abfence, enter, and, affifted with the bayliffs and conftables, ranfack his houfe at *Colchefter*, violently break open his ftudy, and carry away divers of his books, writings, and what elfe the purfivant pleafed, without making reftitution —— that he was then [farther] profecuted in the high commiffion court, principally for his faid book, fined £ 1000 to the king, excommunicated, debarred to practice phyfic

[ordered]

[ordered] to pay coſt of ſuit, and be impriſoned till he ſhould recant, aſſerting that he was thus heavily cenſured only for having maintained the king's prerogative againſt the papacy ; and charging archbiſhop *Laud* with having patronized and defended a book wrote to maintain and defend the papal religion and church of *Rome* ; alledging alſo that at the declaration of the cenſure all the biſhops then preſent denied openly that they held their juriſdiction from the king, affirming that they had it from God only, the archbiſhop maintaining the church of *Rome* to be a true church. He likewiſe further complained, that having thereupon, and for vindicating his innocency as to the matters for which he was unjuſtly cenſured, publiſhed another book in Latin, entitled, *Apologeticus ad preſules Anglicanos,* expreſſing the truth of the proceedings and ſpeeches at his ſaid cenſure, an information was exhibited againſt him and others in the ſtar-chamber for the ſaid book, and another called the *Letany,* not then in print, his anſwer whereunto not being accepted, but the information taken *pro confeſſo,* he was cenſured in £. 5000 to the king, to ſtand in the pillory, and loſe both his ears, and be cloſe impriſoned in *Lanceſton* caſtle, all which was ſeverely executed upon him, to the peril of his life ; after all which he was, by what order he knew not, it being no part of his cenſure, tranſported thence to the iſland of *Scilly,* a place barren, and devoid of common neceſſaries, where he had been cloſe confined above three years, and none of his friends ſuffered to come to him, his wife being by order of the lords of council prohibited under pain of impriſonment, to ſet foot on the iſland ; and that he ſuſtained beſides great ſtraits and miſeries during the ſaid time, all which was contrary to the laws of God and man, and the liberties of a free ſubject, to the utter undoing of him, his wife and children. Whereupon he prayed that honourable aſſembly to take thoſe his preſſing grievances into their conſideration, and to afford him ſuch relief as ſhould ſeem conſonant to juſtice and equity, and to aſſign him counſel, and grant him an order for the neceſſary copies, with a warrant to bring in his witneſſes.

On the ſame day the petitions of *Peter Leigh* and *Richard Golburn* of the city of *Cheſter* were preſented and read. They complained that they had been moſt ſeverely ſentenced in the high commiſſion court at *York* only for viſiting Mr. *Prynn* in his paſſage to *Garnarvan* caſtle. After
all

all thefe petitions had been owned and avowed a large committee was ap-appointed to take them into confideration, who had power to receive all petitions of the like nature, and to confider of the jurifdiction of the high commiffion courts of *Canterbury* and *York*, and of the feveral abufes committed in thofe courts, or by any judges or officers of thofe courts ; and of the court of ftar-chamber, with power to fend for parties, wit-neffes, papers, records, or any thing elfe conducive to the bufinefs, and to affign and hear counfel.   To meet the next day in the ftar-chamber.

Mr. *Lambert Ofbaldfton* [late mafter of *Weftminfter*-fchool] prefented his petition to the houfe of lords, wherein he reprefented that one *Walker* and *Cadwallader Powell*, fervants of the bifhop of *Lincoln* [Dr. *Williams*] fubpœnaed to be defendants in a third information in the ftar-chamber againft the faid bifhop, had, to gratify the archbifhop of *Can-terbury*, and free themfelves from this information, confpired to accufe the petitioner, and did thereupon moft unlawfully break up hampers, and rifle the papers of their lord, then imprifoned in the tower, for letters of the petitioner to him, intercepting other letters fo directed, conveying them all into the hands of *Richard Kilvert*, whom they forced to fhew them to the archbifhop, and put them into an information againft the petitioner ; and that the faid *Walker* alfo produced fome letters or notes of his own lords, tho' exprefs commandment of fecrecy was therein contained, whereby, with his own teftimony, he interpreted the faid letters contrary to the petitioners true fenfe and meaning, as he had feveral times fworn ; and that by this perfidious combination certain words of *Little Urchin* and *Hocus Pocus* ; as alfo of *Great Don* and *Le-viathan*, had been, contrary to the truth, applied to the archbifhop of *Canterbury*, and the lord treafurer ; that he had been fentenced and fined in the ftar-chamber to be deprived and degraded of all his fpiritual pre-ferments, to pay a fine of £. 5000 to his grace, when all his means were taken away—to have his ears nailed to the pillory in the deans yard in *Weftminfter*, before the fcholars whom he had fuccefsfully taught, and to other ignominious punifhments ; and forasmuch as this fentence could not be prevented by the moft humble fubmiffion to his grace before, or by a multitude of petitions and earneft requefts made by the petitioner and his brother to his grace after the fentence was pronounced by their

unjuft

unjuft proceedings, by fuppofing againft law the petitioners letters to have been publifhed by the bifhop of *Lincoln*, tho' there was no proof that the bifhop received them, who upon his oath denied it, nor any man charged to have feen them, and that damages of £.5000 were given to his grace, who was neither plaintiff nor relator in the caufe, by a kind of compliment of the lord keeper • He for thofe great and high concuf-fions in this profecution implored their lordfhips juftice, to have his grievous fentence fufpended til their lordfhips fhould have heard the caufe; his freehold fequeftred; himfelf licenced to profecute his grievances in perfon; and the caufe directed to fuch a courfe of proceeding as fhould feem moft convenient to that honourable affembly.

Echard fays that when Mr. *Ofbaldfton* loft his fchool by means of the fevere fentence in the ftar-chamber [pronounced in Feb. 1638] there were above fourfcore doctors of the three faculties in the two univerfities who gratefully acknowledged their education under him. He efcaped the intended ignominious punifhment, by getting out of court, where he had ftood unobferved, before his fentence was clofed; and going directly to his ftudy at the fchool, after burning fome writings, he left a paper upon his defk whereon he wrote, *If the archbifhop enquire after me, tell him I am gone beyond* Canterbury; whereupon meffengers were fent to the port-towns to apprehend him; but he lay concealed in town till the par-liament met in November 1640.

Bifhop *Williams* was jointly profecuted with Mr. *Ofbaldfton*, they being charged with having plotted together to divulge falfe news and lies, to breed a difturbance in the ftate, and difference between two great perfons and peers of the realm, the late lord treafurer *Wefton*, and the archbifhop of *Canterbury*. Doctor *Williams*, in the latter part of the reign of king *James*, had been confidered as an able ftatefman, and thereupon made lord keeper. In faithfulnefs to his majefty he took the moft favourable opportunity [when his confcience was tender and humble] to fhew him the way of a good king as well as of a good chriftian in thefe points, 1ft. To call parliaments often, to affect them, to accord with them. To which propofal it is faid he fully won his majeftys heart. 2d. To allow his fubjects the liberty and right of the laws, without intrenching by his prerogative; which he attended to with much patience, and repented

he

he had not lookt into that counfel fooner : but on the acceffion of king *Charles* this prelate was held in lefs efteem ; neverthelefs he gave to his majefty fuch faithful and wholefome counfel, as duly confidered might have been attended with happy confequences to himfelf and his kingdom, advifing the obfervance of temperate and conciliating meafures with his firft parliament ; and their adjournment to *Oxford* being propofed in council at. *Hampton-Court*, on the 10th of July 1625, he oppofed this motion with pregnant reafons, which the favorite *Buckingham* treated with fcorn, inftead of examining their force ; but who having gained an unhappy afcendency over the kings judgment as well as affections his in-fluence over ruled all objections, in confequence whereof the parliament continued their feffion at *Oxford* on the firft of Auguft following, where complaints, chiefly againft the favorite, with fharp contefts, enfuing, " the commons were by the court, then at *Woodftock*, cenfured for fpite-" ful and feditious, therefore not fit to continue, but to be diffolved. " Which refolution being brought to the clerk of the crown to diffolve " them on the 12th of Auguft," bifhop *Hacket* fays, " the Keeper did " never fo beftir him fince he was born, as to turn the tide, with reafons, " with fupplications, with tears, imploring his majefty to remember a " time when, in his hearing, his bleffed father had charged him to call " parliaments often, and continue them, though their rafhnefs fometimes " did offend him ; that in his own experience he never got good by " falling out with them. *But chiefly, Sir,* fays he, *let it never be faid* " *that you have not kept good correfpondence with your firft parliament. Do* " *not diffeminate fo much unkindnefs through all the counties and boroughs* " *of your realm. The love of your people is the palladium of your crown.* " *Continue this affembly to another feffion, and expect alteration for the* " *better. If you do not fo, the next fwarm will come out of the fame hive.* " To this the lords of the council did almoft all concur ; but it wanted " *Buckinghams* fuffrage ; who was fecure that the kings judgment would " follow him againft all the table. So this parliament was blafted, *et* " *radicis vitium in fructibus nafcentibus oftenditur.* The root failed, and " the fruit was unfavoury in all the branches that grew up after it." Before the diffolution of the parliament was confidered in council the Keeper had likewife given to *Buckingham* the beft advice, ufing the moft

cogent

cogent arguments to diffuade him from this defign, advifing that a fair and friendly promife fhould be made to the members of their meeting again after *Chriftmas*, and that he fhould requite injuries with benefits, faying, " no man that is wife will be angry with the people of *England*," at the fame time renewing his former counfel, that he fhould make a more prudent and moderate ufe of his power; and in conclufion telling him that, if he liked not this advice, truth would in time find an advocate. The duke replied, " I will look whom I truft to," and flung out of the chamber with a menacing countenance, his ambition overcoming his reafon, and his boundlefs confidence in the kings favour having rendered him fo imperious, that he was incapable of falutary advice; yet fuch is the condition of human affairs, we find, under the beft form of government, when the true fpirit of it is loft, that the honour, fafety and welfare of the king and kingdom were become dependent on the will of this improvident man, the king being, unhappily, fo far prejudiced in his favour that, having through his influence declared war againft *France*, in order to maintain it, he was appointed captain general and admiral, with the command of an army and fleet, though a ftranger to military fervice by fea and land; his ill fuccefs, with the national lofs and difgrace, being fuitable to his prefumption and his talents; but infufficient to efface the royal prejudices; and, though devoid of found policy, being efteem'd by his majefty, as well as by his adherents and fycophants, a great ftatefman, under pretence of maintaining the royal prerogative, he boldly invaded the public rights, and, with his partifans, created fuch breaches between the king and his parliaments as were never healed, his intention being to eftablifh an abfolute power in the king, in order that, in his name, he might be the real mafter, and govern all things according to his own will, and by his own conduct giving the houfe of commons ample reafon to declare, in their remonftrance to his majefty, that the principal caufe of the evils and dangers of the kingdom was his exceffive power, and his abufe of it; and no prince in *Europe* could, I conceive, by profecuting the fharpeft war againft king *Charles* have become fo dangerous to him as this favourite was, who by his great influence mifguiding his actions, and over ruling all wifer counfels, and for the fake of his own fafety and aggrandifement, encreafing and confirming the errors

touching

touching the regal power which this prince had imbibed in his fathers court, dishonoured and embarrassed him, distressing his affairs both at home and abroad, disgusted his parliaments, broke up the common tranquillity, and by his whole conduct caused the diminution, or alienation of the peoples affections, which are ever the chief safety as well as the glory of the prince.

In October following the great seal was taken from doctor *Williams*, without the least pretence of any miscarriage in him, and in compliance with the kings pleasure acquiescing in his desired absence from the next parliament he was not without difficulty admitted to appear even by proxy; but this parliament, after having spent the best part of eighteen weeks in forming and prosecuting their complaints against the duke, being dissolved, and public affairs growing daily more and more interesting, when the third parliament was called he determined to maintain the right of his peerage; but the lord keeper *Coventry*, by the kings order, attempting to stop him, if possible, by letter, wherein he signified the king's pleasure to this effect, he conducted the matter so that the peers called for his assistance, whereupon he gave his attendance, and in the course of the session he opposed the loan demanded of the subject contrary to the laws: and two sermons having been preached before the king by Dr. *Manwaring*, one of his chaplains, which were published by his majesty's special command, wherein he attempted to establish an absolute power in the king, with active and passive obedience in the subject, upon pain of damnation, he with great strength of argument exposed the fallacious reasoning of this court sycophant. He likewise strenuously supported the petition of right; and the king having, in order to defeat it, sent his letter to the lords containing in appearance sundry concessions, by judicious observations and sound reasons he shewed that the same were conceived in such general and ambiguous terms that they left to the subject no security of enjoying their liberty and the laws; whereupon these concessions were waved as unsatisfactory.

Echard, after setting forth the various illegal and violent measures taken by the court to enforce the loan, and mentioning the removal of Sir *Randolph Crew* from the place of lord chief justice, by reason of shewing himself dissatisfied with it, and the appointment of Sir

Nicholas

Nicholas Hide, a creature of the duke in his stead, says " The politic
" bishop of *Lincoln* could not wholly escape in this critical juncture;
" who delivering his thoughts concerning the loan, a complaint was sent
" up to the lords of the council, and upon this occasion an information
" of other pretended matters was afterwards preferred against him in the
" star-chamber;" and afterwards, that all the spiritual and temporal
lords about *London* being invited to the grand solemnity of baptizing the
kings first born son, " only the declining bishop of *Lincoln* was design-
" edly omitted; which with great uneasiness caused him to ask the reason
" of the earl of *Holland*; who freely told him, *That he must expect worse*
" *than this, because he was such a champion for* the petition of right; *that*
" *there was no room at the table for those that liked it.*" And in relating
the proceedings of the government in the year 1637, after mentioning
the severe censures of Dr. *Bastwick* and others, which occasioned great
disgust, he writes thus. " Before these last proceedings were fully
" finished there came on the famous cause in the star-chamber, against
" a far greater man, Dr. *Williams*, bishop of *Lincoln*, which had dif-
" ferent, tho' no less remarkable effects."—" The king and the arch-
" bishop had entertained insuperable prejudices against him, and look'd
" upon him as a dangerous affector of popularity, and a favourite of
" the *Puritan* faction."—" The begining of his troubles arose from Sir
" *John Lamb* and Dr. *Sibthorp*, who with *Allen* and *Burden*, two
" proctors, being at dinner with him at *Buckden*, there began a discourse
" concerning non-conformists. Now the bishop, knowing these to be
" all active men in the prosecution of them, advised them to abate their
" severity, for he knew the king would treat them more mildly for the
" future, being a considerable party that much influenced parliamentary
" affairs; adding further, *That the King had communicated this to him*
" *with his own mouth.* A few years after, upon some difference with the
" bishop, Sir *John Lamb* and Dr. *Sibthorp* informed against him in the
" star-chamber for revealing the kings secrets. But the information be-
" ing either not well laid, or sufficiently supported, the bishop, by eva-
" sions, and delays, found means to fence against it for some years
" together; but with great vexation and expense. In the mean time the
" displeasure of the court encreased against him, so that he was daily
" put

" put to some new trouble, and not suffered to have any rest. This
" caused him to apply himself to the lord *Cottington*, and beg *to*
" *know how he might procure his peace, and such ordinary favours as other*
" *bishops had from his majesty.*   That lord advised him to two things, to
" resign his deanery of *Westminster*, and to restrain his great and magni-
" ficent way of living ; both which he refused, the former out of good
" reason, and the latter out of a resolute temper.

" At length *Kilvert*, a proctor in the *Arches*, a person very scandalous
" and cunning, who before had been employed in hunting *Bennet*, a cor-
" rupt judge in the *prerogative*, to his final sentence, was retained by
" some great men to prosecute this bishop to the like confusion. This
" man having found by diligent enquiry, and subtle practices, that the
" bishops purgation depended chiefly upon one *Prigeon*, the register of
" the court of *Lincoln*, he made it his chief business by discrediting the
" witness to invalidate his evidence, and so laid a bastard to his charge,
" there appearing a sufficient ground for an indictment against him. The
" bishop apprehending himself under a necessity to support the reputa-
" tion of *Prigeon*, engaged himself more zealously than was thought
" consistent with the dignity of so great a prelate for so inconsiderable
" a man. He was at a vast expense to ward off the blow, and the
" fathering of the bastard was bandied between *Prigeon* and one *Booth*
" from session to session, and from one year to another, till the mother
" of the child was found to have been tampered with by some of the
" bishops creatures to charge it wholly upon *Booth*, who, when it was
" too late, actually owned himself to be the true father. On the dis-
" covery of which practice *Kilvert* let go his former hold, and exhibited
" a new bill against the bishop for *tampering with the kings witnesses*, a
" crime most proper for the star-chamber. The bishop finding himself
" plunged into new difficulties, and under the weight of a merciless
" persecution, endeavoured to obtain a composition with the king, be-
" ing willing to pay four, and then eight thousand pounds to purchase
" his own peace, and his majesty's favour ; which tho' for a while ac-
" cepted of, afterwards was urged against him, as a proof of his con-
" sciousness and guilt of the crime charged upon him.

" About

" About the middle of *July* the cause came to a full hearing, which
" held nine days debate, with an extraordinary concourse of people,
" who highly pitied the bishop, as a man marked out for a sacrifice to
" the court, and one who was like to bleed in his purse towards a de-
" signed war against *Scotland*. In conclusion he was condemned to ten
" thousand pounds fine to the king, a thousand marks to Sir *John Moun-*
" *fon*, who was concerned against *Prigeon*, suspension in the high com-
" mission [b] from all office and benefice, and imprisonment during his
" majestys pleasure. All this was executed without the least abatement;
" and *Walker* his secretary, *Powell* his steward, and one *Land*, were
" severally fined, and ordered to be imprisoned: but they all escaped
" both fine and imprisonment, which were in a short time commuted
" into such other offices as they were to do for *Kilvert* against their
" master, as he soon found to his new perlexity and damage: for after
" the bishop had been imprisoned in the tower, and had his goods to a
" vast value shamefully wasted by *Kilvert* at *Buckden*, in the rifling of
" his papers, *Powel* found a letter writ to him about five years before,
" by Mr. *Osbaldston* the school-master of *Westminster*, in which there
" were some enigmatical expressions, which were thought highly reflect-
" ing upon the archbishop and the then lord treasurer *Weston*. This be-
" ing produced *Kilvert* took the advantage, and exhibited a new bill
" against him for *divulging scandalous libels against privy-counsellors*. The
" bishop denied that ever he had received the letter, but it being found
" in a box in his chamber, with another paper that seemed fully to ex-
" plain it, he was condemned in another fine of eight thousand pounds."
According to *Rushworth* the sentence of the court was, " That the
" bishop of *Lincoln* should be fined in £. 5000 to the king, and £. 3000
" to the archbishop; to be imprisoned during the king's pleasure, and
" to make submission." By force of the preceding sentences he continued a prisoner in the tower until the 16th of November 1640, when,
Rushworth says, he " was sent for to take his place in the house of lords,

[b] He was sentenced to pay a fine of £ 10000 to the king, to be imprisoned in the tower
during his majestys pleasure, and to be suspended from all his ecclesiastical functions, both *ab
officio & beneficio*, and was referred to the high commission court to censure him as they should
think fit concerning his degrees, as particularly appears in *Rushworth*.

" his

" his majefty having by a gracious meffage fignified that it fhould be fo,
" without an enquiry into, or repetition of, what had formerly paffed.
" For there being much bufinefs to be done his majefty was willing there
" fhould be a full houfe." The bifhop being reftored to his feat in parliament, it is needlefs to fay that he was able fully to reprefent the manifold grievous oppreffions which he had fuffered from the court of ftar-
chamber; but it may be remembered that the archbifhop in giving judgment againft him, in July 1637, cited feveral parts of the *civil* law, and
from the *canon* law divers councils, with the decretals, in fupport of it.

1640-1.   On the 22d of *Febr.* Mr. *Rigby* reported " from the committee for
" high commiffion and ftar-chamber court the cafe of Dr. *Baftwick*;
" whereupon it was refolved, That the precept made by the archbifhop
" of *Canterbury* and others, high commiffioners for caufes ecclefiaftical
" within the realm of *England*, for the apprehending of the body of Dr.
" *Baftwick*, and in fearching for and feizing his books; and the mef-
" fengers actings thereupon in fearching Dr. *Baftwicks* houfe, and feiz-
" ing his books and papers, are againft law, and the liberty of the
" fubject."

" Refolved &c. That the fentence given againft Dr. *Baftwick* by the
" high commiffioners, and the proceedings whereupon that fentence is
" grounded, and the execution of that fentence, are againft law; and
" that the fentence is void, and that Dr. *Baftwick* ought to be reftored to
" the exercife and practice of phyfic, and to have reparation and recom-
" penfe for his damage and lofs, fuftained by the faid fentence and exe-
" cution."

" Refolved &c. That all thofe feveral commiffioners of the high-com-
" miffion court, which voted againft Dr. *Baftwick* in the fentence pro-
" nounced againft him, ought to give fatisfaction to Dr. *Baftwick*.

The Houfe afterwards refumed the debate concerning Dr. *Baftwick*;
whereupon it was further

" Refolved &c. That the proceedings againft Dr. *Baftwick* [in the
" court of Star-chamber] are againft the law and the liberty of the fub-
" ject, as alfo the fentence againft him ought to be reverfed, the fine of
" £.5000 difcharged, and he to have reparation for his loffes and fuf-
" ferings."

" Refolved

" Refolved &c. That the orders and warrants from the council-board
" for Dr. *Baftwicks* exile, and transferring from the caftle of *Lancefton*
" to the ifle of *Scilly*, and his imprifonment there, are againft the law
" and liberty of the fubject, and that he ought to have reparation for his
" loffes and damages fuftained by thofe orders, and that imprifon-
" ment [c].

On the 5th of March 1640 Lord *Andover* made the following fpeech.

" My Lords,
" Since your lordfhips have already looked fo far into privileges of
" peers as to make a ftrict inquifition upon foreign honours, let us not
" deftroy That among ourfelves which we defire to preferve from
" ftrangers."
" And if this grievance I fhall move againft have flept til now, it is
" very confiderable, left cuftom make it every day more apparent than
" other. Your lordfhips very well know that there was a ftatute framed,
" 3 *Hen.* VII. authorizing the chancellor, treafurer, and privy feal, and
" the two chief juftices, calling to them one bifhop, and a temporal
" lord of the kings council, to receive complaints upon bill or infor-
" mation, and cite fuch parties to appear as ftand accufed of any mifde-
" meanor ; and this was the infancy of the ftar-chamber : but after-
" wards the ftar-chamber was, by cardinal *Wolfey*, 8 *Hen.* VIII. raifed to
" mans eftate ; from whence (being now altogether unlimited) it is
" grown a monfter, and will hourly produce worfe effects, unlefs it be
" reduced by that hand which laid the foundation ; for the ftatutes
" which are ratified by parliament admit of no other than a repeal.
" Therefore I offer humbly to your lordfhips thefe enfuing reafons why it
" fhould be repealed."
" Firft, The very words of the ftatute clearly fhew that it was a *need-*
" *lefs inftitution* ; for it fays, They who are to judge, can proceed with
" no delinquent otherwife than if he were convicted of the fame crime
" by due procefs of law. And do your lordfhips hold this a rational court,

[c] *Rufhworths* Collec⁵. vol. iv. p. 193. and State Tryals, vol. i. p. 482.

" that

" that fends us to the law, and calls us to the law, and calls us back
" from it again ?"

" Secondly, Divers judicatories confound one another, *et in peſſima
" republica plurimæ leges.*"

" The third reafon is from circumftance, or rather *à conſuetudine ;*
" and of this there are many examples both domeftic and foreign; but
" more particularly by the parliaments of *France,* abbreviated into a
" ftanding committee by *Philip* the king, and continued according to his
" inftitution until *Lewis* XI came to the crown; who being a fubtle
" prince, buried the volume in the epitome; for to this day, whenever
" the three eftates are called, either at the death of the old king, or to
" crown the new, it is a common proverb, *allons voire le feu des eſtats :*
" My lords, arbitrary judgments deftroy the common laws, and in them
" the two great charters of the kingdom; which being once loft we have
" nothing left but the name of liberty."

" Then the laft reafon is (though it was the firft caufe of my ftanding
" up) the great eclipfe it hath ever been to the whole nobility; for
" who are fo frequently vexed there as peers and noblemen? and not-
" withftanding their appeal to this affembly is ever good, whilft that
" famous law, of 4 *Edw.* III. remains in force, for the holding of a par-
" liament once a year, or more, if occafion require; yet who durft a
" year ago mention fuch a ftatute, without incurring the danger of Mr.
" *Kilverts* perfecution? Therefore I fhall humbly move your lordfhips,
" That a felect committee of a few may be named, to confider of the
" act of parliament itsfelf; and if they fhall think it of as great pre-
" judice as I do, that then the houfe of commons, in the moft ufual
" manner, may be made acquainted with it, either by bill or conference,
" who alfo haply think it a burden to the fubject; and fo when the
" whole body of parliament fhall join in one fupplication, I am confident
" his majefty will defire that nothing fhall remain in force which his
" people do not willingly obey [*d*]."

[*d*] *Ruſhworths* Collect'. vol, iv, p. 204,

On

On the 12th of March, Mr. *Rigby* reported the cafe of Mr. *Burton*; whereupon it was " Refolved, That the four commiffioners, Dr. *Duck,* " Dr. *Worral,* Dr. *Sams,* and Dr. *Wood,* proceeded unjuftly and illegally " in fufpending Mr. *Burton ab officio & beneficio,* for not appearing upon " the fummons the firft procefs."

" Secondly, That the breaking up Mr. *Burtons* houfe, and arrefting " his perfon without any caufe fhewed, and before any fuit depended " againft him in the ftar-chamber, and his clofe imprifonment thereupon, " are againft the law and liberty of the fubject."

" Thirdly, that *John Wragg* hath offended in fearching and feizing " the books and papers of Mr. *Burton,* by colour of a general warrant " dormant from the high commiffioners; and that the faid warrant is " againft law, and the liberty of the fubject; and that ferjeant *Dendy,* " and alderman *Abel* have offended in breaking open the houfe of Mr. " *Burton,* and ought refpectively to make him reparations for the " fame."

" Refolved, That Mr. *Burton* ought to have reparation and recom- " penfe for damages fuftained by the aforefaid proceedings from Dr. " *Duck,* &c."

" Refolved, That the warrant from the council-board, dated at *White-* " *hall, Feb.* 2, 1636, for the committing Mr. *Burton* clofe prifoner, and " the commitment thereupon, is illegal, and contrary to the liberty of " the fubject."

" Refolved, That the archbifhop of *Canterbury,* bifhop of *London,* " and the earl of *Arundel,* the earl of *Pembroke,* Sir *Henry Vane,* fecre- " tary *Cooke,* and fecretary *Windebank,* do make reparation to Mr. " *Burton* for his damages fuftained by this imprifonment [e]."

And on the 24th of March, " The bufinefs of Mr. *Burton* coming " again into confideration, it was refolved, That the fentence in the " ftar-chamber againft Mr. *Burton* is illegal, and without any juft " ground, and ought to be reverfed, and he ought to be freed from the " fine of £. 5000, and imprifonment, impofed by the faid fentence,

[e] *Rufhworths* Collect. vol. iv. p. 207.

" and

" and to be reftored to his degrees taken in the univerfity, orders in the
" miniftry, and to his ecclefiaftical benefice in Friday-ftreet, *London*."

" That the order of the council-board for transferring the faid Mr.
" *Burton* from the caftle of *Lancafter*, to the ifle of *Guernfey*, and imprifon-
" ing him there, are againft the law and liberty of the fubject. That the
" faid Mr. *Burton* ought to have reparation and recompenfe for the
" damages fuftained by the faid imprifonment, lofs of his ears, and other
" evils fuftained by the faid unjuft and illegal proceedings [*f*]."

On the 20th of April a report being made in Mr. *Prynns* cafe it was
refolved upon the queftion,

" 1. That the fentence againft Mr. *Prynn* in the ftar-chamber, Febru-
" ary 17, anno 9 *Car.* is illegal, and given without juft caufe, and ought
" to be reverfed ; and that Mr. *Prynn* ought to be difcharged of the fine
" of £. 5000 impofed by the faid fentence, and of all extents thereupon,
" and of his imprifonment, decreed by that fentence."

" 2. Refolved That Mr. *Prynn* ought to be reftored to his degrees in
" the univerfity of *Oxford*, and to the fociety of *Lincolns-inn*, and to the
" exercife of his profeffion of an utter barrifter at law, and to his chamber
" again at *Lincolns-inn*."

" 3. Refolved, That Mr. *Prynn* ought to have reparation for fuch
" damages and prejudice as he hath fuftained by the faid fentence and
" proceedings."

" 4. Refolved &c. That the fentence given againft Mr. *Prynn* in the
" the ftar-chamber, 14 *Junii* 1637. *Anno* 13 *Car.* is illegal, and given
" without any juft caufe, and therefore ought to be reverfed ; and that
" he ought to be difcharged of the fine and imprifonment thereby de-
" creed ; and that he ought to have reparation and recompenfe for the
" damages fuftained by that fentence, and the execution thereof."

" 5. That the warrant, dated 27 Aug. 13 *Car.* for the tranfportation
" of Mr. *Prynn* from *Carnarvan* caftle to the ifle of *Jerfey*, and his im-
" prifonment there, and other reftraints therein mentioned, are againft
" the law and liberty of the fubject ; and that he ought to be difcharged

[*f*] Id. ibid. p. 213.

" of

" of that imprifonment, and to have reparations for the damages fuf-
" tained thereby."

" 6. Refolved, &c. That the imprifonment of Mr. *Prynn* by a warrant,
" dated 1ft Feb. 1632, under the hands of *Thomas* lord *Coventry*, lord
" keeper of the great feal of *England, Richard* lord archbifhop of *York*,
" *Henry* earl of *Manchefter*, *Edward* earl of *Dorfet*, *Henry* lord vifcount
" *Faulkland*, *William* lord bifhop of *London*, *Edward* lord *Newburgh*,
" and Sir *Thomas Jermin*, is unjuft and illegal, and that they ought to
" give Mr. *Prynn* fatisfaction for the damages fuftained by his imprifon-
" ment."

" It was further ordered, That a charge be drawn up againft Dr.
" *Heylin* touching the promoting the fuit in ftar-chamber againft Mr.
" *Prynn* [g]."

Befides the petitions aforementioned Dr. *Alexander Leighton*, a *Scotch*
divine, on the 7th of November 1640, prefented his petition to the houfe
of commons, complaining of the fevere proceedings againft him in the
ftar-chamber, for writing a book entitled, " An Appeal to the Parlia-
" ment, or A Plea againft Prelacy," whereupon the proper orders were
given touching the profecution of this complaint; and on the 21ft of
April Mr. *Roufe* having reported his cafe, it was refolved upon the
queftion,

" 1. That the attacking, imprifoning and detaining Dr. *Leighton* in
" prifon, by warrant from the high commiffioners, is illegal."

" 2. Refolved, &c. That the breaking up of Dr. *Leightons* houfe, and
" the taking away his papers by *Edward Wright*, then fheriff of *London*,
" and now lord mayor, is illegal."

" 3. Refolved, &c. That the faid *Edward Wright*, then fheriff, and
" now lord mayor of *London*, ought to give reparations to Dr. *Leighton*
" for his damages fuftained by the breaking open his houfe, and taking
" away his papers and other goods, as aforefaid."

" 4. Refolved, &c. That the archbifhop of *Canterbury*, then bifhop
" of *London*, ought to give fatisfaction to Dr. *Leighton* for his damages
" fuftained by fifteen weeks imprifonment in *Newgate*, upon the faid
" bifhops warrant."

[g] *Rufhworths* Collect. vol. iv. p. 228.

" fuftained

" 5. Refolved, &c. That the great fine of £. 10000 laid upon Dr.
" *Leighton*, by fentence in the ftar-chamber, is illegal."

" 6. Refolved, &c. That the fentence of corporal punifhment im-
" pofed upon Dr. *Leighton*, the whiping, branding, fliting the nofe,
" cutting off his ears, fetting in the pillory, and the execution thereof,
" and imprifonment thereupon, are illegal."

" 7. Refolved, &c. That Dr. *Leighton* ought to be freed from the great
" fine of £. 10000, and from the fentence of perpetual imprifonment, and
" to have his bonds delivered to him, which he entered into for his true
" imprifonment."

" 8. Refolved, &c. That Dr. *Leighton* ought to have good fatisfaction
" and reparation for his great fufferings and damages fuftained by the
" illegal fentences in the ftar-chamber [*b*]."

John Lilburne, clofe prifoner in the fleet, likewife, on the 7th of November 1640, prefented his petition to the houfe of commons, complaining of the proceedings againft him in the ftar-chamber in February
1637-8, for printing and publifhing of libellous and feditious books,
intitled, " News from *Ipfwich*, &c." contrary to a decree of that court
made in July preceding, to prohibit the printing of books without licenfe, to this effect,

" That none fhall prefume to print any book or pamphlet whatfoever,
" unlefs the fame be firft licenfed, with all the titles, epiftles and pre-
" faces therewith imprinted, by the lord archbifhop of *Canterbury*, or
" the bifhop of *London* for the time being, or by their appointment, and
" within the limits of either univerfity, by the chancellor or vice-chan-
" cellor thereof, upon pain that every printer fo offending fhall for ever
" thereafter be difabled to exercife the art of printing, and fhall fuffer
" fuch further punifhment as by this court, or the high-commiffion, fhall
" be thought fitting ; that before any books imported from foreign parts
" fhall be expofed to fale, a true catalogue thereof fhall be prefented to
" the archbifhop of *Canterbury*, or the bifhop of *London*: And that no
" officers of the cuftom fhall deliver any foreign books out of their hands
" and cuftody, before thofe bifhops fhall have appointed one of their

[*b*] *Rufhworths* Collect. vol. iv. p. 228, 229.

" chaplains,

" chaplains, or fome other learned man, with the mafter and wardens
" of the company of ftationers, or one of them, to be prefent at the
" opening of the pack and fardels, and to view the fame. And thofe
" that difobey this injunction are to be cenfured in this or the high-
" commiffion court, as the feveral caufes fhall require. And if in this
" fearch there happen to be found any fchifmatical or offenfive books,
" they fhall be brought to the aforefaid bifhops, or the high-commiffion
" office, that the offenders may be punifhed. That no perfon whatfo-
" ever fhall imprint in the parts beyond the fea, or import from thence,
" any Englifh books, or whereof the greater part is *Englifh*, whether
" formerly printed or not. And that no books whatfoever fhall be re-
" printed, though formerly licenfed, without a new licenfe firft obtained,
" upon pain of like cenfure and punifhment. And that if any perfon
" whatfoever, that is not an allowed printer, fhall prefume to fet up a
" prefs for printing, or work at any fuch prefs, or fet and compofe letters
" for the fame, he fhall be fet in the pillory, and whipt through the city
" of *London* [*i*].'

Here we find the court of ftar-chamber, in manifeft derogation of
the legiflative authority of the kingdom, and in open violation of the
rights of the fubject, making laws reftrictive, or rather fubverfive of
civil and religious liberty, with fevere penal fanctions, according to their
fovereign will, fubjecting offenders againft them to punifhment at the difcretion of this court, or of the high-oommiffion, without limitation of
nature or number ; and what feverities their difcretion dictated we have
in fome meafure fhewn.

Upon the profecution of *Lilburne* he was ordered to be examined,
upon interrogatories, touching the matters charged upon him ; and being
brought up to the office for examination he refufed to take an oath to
anfwer interrogatories, faying it was the oath *ex officio*, and that no free-
born *Englifhman* ought to take it; not being bound by the law to accufe
himfelf. And afterwards, upon the 9th of February, peremptorily refufing to take the oath tendered to him in open court, he was remanded
to the fleet, to remain clofe prifoner until he fhould take his oath, and

[*i*] *Rufhworths* Collect. vol. iv. p. 463, 464.

be

be examined. And it was by the court declared that unlefs he fhould fubmit to take the oath, and be examined, by a certain appointed time, their lordfhips would on the laft fitting of the term proceed to cenfure him for his contempt. And on the 13th of the fame month appearing again in court, the attorney general informed their lordfhips that he had obftinately continued his refufal, and moved them to pafs cenfure upon him for his contempt; whereupon their lordfhips endeavoured to per-fuade him to conform, offering then to accept his oath, without proceed-ing to cenfure; but ftill perfifting in his refufal to take the oath propofed, " the whole court did with unanimous confent declare and adjudge the " faid *Lilburne* guilty of a very high contempt and offence, of danger-" ous consequence and evil example, and worthy to undergo a very fharp, " fevere, and exemplary cenfure, which might deter others from the " like prefumptuous boldnefs in refufing to take a legal oath, without " which many grievous and exorbitant offences, to the prejudice and " danger of his majefty, his kingdoms and loving fubjects, might go " away undifcovered and unpunifhed." And therefore their lordfhips decreed that he fhould be remanded to the fleet, there to remain til he fhould obey the orders of the court, and pay a fine of £. 500 to his majeftys ufe; and before his enlargement to become bound with good fureties for his good behaviour; and the more to deter others from offend-ing in the like kind, they further decreed that he fhould be whipt from the prifon of the fleet to the pillory, to be erected when and where they fhould direct; and that he fhould be fet in the pillory, and from thence be returned to the fleet, there to remain according to their decree.

On the 18th of April following, in execution of this fentence, he was feverely whipt from the fleet to *Weftminfter:* During his whiping and ftanding in the pillory he uttered many bold fpeeches againft the tyranny of bifhops, &c. and when his head was in the pillory he fcattered among the people fundry copies of pamphlets, faid to be feditious, of which the court of ftar-chamber, then fitting, being informed they immediately ordered him to be gagged during the refidue of the time appointed for his ftanding in the pillory, which was accordingly done; upon which he ftamped with his feet, thereby intimating to the beholders, as *Rufh-*
worth

worth fuppofes, he would ftill fpeak were his mouth at liberty; and on the fame day the court of ftar-chamber made the following order.

" Whereas *John Lilburne*, prifoner in the fleet, by fentence in ftar-
" chamber, did this day fuffer condign punifhment for his feveral offen-
" ces, by whiping at a cart, and ftanding in the pillory, and (as their
" lordfhips were this day informed) during the time that his body was
" under the faid execution, audacioufly and wickedly, not only uttered
" fundry fcandalous and feditious fpeeches, but likewife fcattered fundry
" copies of feditious books amongft the people that beheld the faid exe-
" cution, for which very thing, amongft other offences of like nature,
" he had been cenfured in the faid court by the aforefaid fentence. It
" was thereupon ordered by their lordfhips that the faid *Lilburne* fhould
" be laid alone with irons on his hands and legs in the wards of the fleet,
" where the bafeft and meaneft fort of prifoners are ufed to be put, and
" that the warden of the fleet take fpecial care to hinder the refort of any
" perfon whatfoever unto him, and particularly that he be not fupplied
" with any hand, and that he take fpecial notice of all letters, writings,
" and books brought unto him, and feize and deliver the fame unto
" their lordfhips; and take notice from time to time who they be that
" refort to the faid prifon to vifit the faid *Lilburne*, or to fpeak with him,
" and inform the board [*k*]." And on that day their lordfhips made this
" farther order.

" That his majeftys attorney and follicitor general be hereby prayed
" and required to take ftrict examination of *John Lilburne*, prifoner in
" the fleet, touching the demeanour and fpeeches of him the faid *Lil-*
" *burne* during the time of his whiping and ftanding in the pillory this
" day, according to fentence of his majeftys court of ftar-chamber, par-
" ticularly, whether the faid *Lilburne* did at that time utter any fpeeches
" tending to fedition, or to the difhonour of the faid court of ftar-
" chamber, or any member of the faid court? And whether he did
" throw about and difperfe at the fame time any feditious pamphlets and
" books, either of that fort for which he was formerly cenfured, or any
" other of the like nature? What the fpeeches were, and who heard

[*k*] *Rufhworth*, vol. ii. p. 466.

" them

"d them ? What the faid books were, and whence, and of whom the faid
" *Lilburne* had them ? And what other material circumftances they
" fhall think fit to examine either the faid *Lilburne* upon, or any other
" perfon by whom they fhall think good to inform themfelves for the
" better finding out the truth : and thereupon to make certificate to the
" board what they find, together with their opinions [*l*]."

Lilburne having for fome time lain with double irons on his hands
and feet in the inner wards of the prifon, a fire happened near the place
in which he was clofe confined, which gave a jealoufie that in his fury
and anguifh of pain he was defperate, and had fet the prifon on fire, not
regarding himfelf to be burnt with it : the neighbouring inhabitants
without the fleet, and the prifoners within all cried, *releafe* Lilburne, *or
we fhall all be burnt* ; whereupon they run headlong, and made the
warden remove him out of his hold, and the fire was quenched, and he
remained a prifoner in a place where he had fome more air.   He continued in prifon to the time of prefenting his petition, when it was or-
derered,   " That he fhould have liberty, by warrant of this houfe, to go
" abroad in fafe cuftody, to profecute his petition exhibited here ; and
" that he be removed out of the common prifon where now he is, into
" fome more convenient place, and have the liberty of the fleet [*m*]."

The houfe of commons conceiving *John Lilburnes* cafe proper for
the confideration of the houfe of lords, they tranfmitted the fame to their
lordfhips, who after all proper proceedings, made the following order
thereupon.

" Whereas the caufe of *John Lilburne* gent. came this day to a hear-
" ing at the bar, by his counfel, being tranfmitted from the houfe of
" commons, concerning a fentence pronounced againft him in the ftar-
" chamber Feb. 13th *Anno* 13 *Car. regis* ; and after an examination of
" the whole proceedings, and a due confideration of the faid fentence,
" it is this day adjudged, ordered, and determined by the lords in par-
" liament affembled, that the faid fentence, and all proceedings there-
" upon, fhall forthwith be for ever totally vacuated, obliterated, and
" taken off the file in all courts where they are yet remaining, as illegal,

[*l*] *Rufhworth*, vol. ii. p. 467.   [*m*] Id. vol. iv. p. 20.

" and

" and moft unjuft, againft the liberty of the fubject, and the law of the
" land, and *magna charta*, and unfit to continue upon record; and that
" the faid *Lilburne* fhall be for ever abfolutely freed, and totally dif-
" charged from the faid fentence, and all proceedings thereupon, as fully
" and amply as though never any fuch thing had been. And that all
" eftreats and procefs in the courts of exchequer for levying of any
" fine (if any fuch be) fhall be wholly cancelled and made void, any
" thing to the contrary in any wife notwithftanding."

John Brown, Cler. Parliament [n].

On the 4th of May 1641, Mr. *Roufe* reported the cafe of *John Lilburne*, whereupon it was,

" 1. Refolved, That the fentence in the ftar-chamber given againft
" *John Lilburne* is illegal, and againft the liberty of the fubject, and
" alfo bloody, wicked, cruel [o], and tyrannical."

" 2. Refolved, That reparation ought to be given to Mr. *Lilburne* for
" his imprifonment, fuffering, and loffes, fuftained by that illegal fen-
" tence [p]."

Lord *Clarendon* gives the following account of the proceedings in parliament for abolifhing the court of ftar-chamber.

" A bill for taking away the ftar-chamber court. The progrefs of
" which bill was this. The exorbitances of this court had been fuch
" (as hath been before touched) that there were very few perfons of
" quality who had not fuffered, or been perplexed, by the weight or

[n] *Rufhorth*, vol. ii. p. 469.

[o] On the hearing before the Lords it was faid that, " clofe imprifonment was never ufed
" to the primitive chriftians by any tyrant; for then that heavy charge in Scripture, *I was in
" prifon, and ye vifited me not*, might be anfwered; but a clofe imprifonment may prefume a
" famifhment, and fo death. The *Romans* had four punifhments, *lapidatio, combuftio, decolla-
" tio*, and *ftrangulatio*; but never famifhing to death. This man might have been fo, as it
" was fworn."

" Three years imprifonment till the parliament releafed him, and might otherwife have been
" for ever." *Rufhworth*, vol. ii. p. 468.

[p] Id. vol. iv. p. 250.

" fear

" fear of thofe cenfures and judgments.   For having extended their ju-
" rifdiction from riots, perjury, and the moſt notorious miſdemeanors,
" to an aſſerting all proclamations and orders of ſtate; to the vindica-
" ting illegal commiſſions, and grants of monopolies (all which were
" the chief ground-works of their late proceedings) no man could hope
" to be longer free from the inquiſition of that court than he reſolved
" to ſubmit to thoſe, and the like extraordinaay courſes.   And therefore
" there was an entire inclination to limit and regulate the proceedings
" of that court, to which purpoſe a bill was brought in, and twice
" read, and, according to cuſtom, committed.   It being returned after
" by the committee, and the amendments read, it was ſuddenly ſug-
" geſted (by a perſon not at all enclined to confuſion, or to the violent
" party that intended that confuſion) *that the remedies provided by that*
" *bill were not proportionable to the diſeaſes; that the uſurpations of that*
" *court were not leſs in the forms of their proceedings than in the matter*
" *upon which they proceeded; inſomuch that the courſe of the court (which*
" *is the rule of their judging) was ſo much corrupted, that the grievance*
" *was as much thereby, in thoſe caſes of which they had a proper connu-*
" *ſance, as it was by their exceſs in holding pleas of that in which, in truth,*
" *they had no juriſdiction; and therefore he conceived the proper and moſt*
" *natural cure for that miſchief would be utterly to aboliſh that court,*
" *which it was very difficult, if not impoſſible, to regulate; and in place*
" *thereof to erect and eſtabliſh ſuch a juriſdiction as might be thought ne-*
" *ceſſary.*   Hereupon the ſame bill was recommitted, with direction, *ſo*
" *far to alter the frame of it as might ſerve utterly to take away and aboliſh*
" *that court;* which was accordingly done, and again brought to the
" houſe, and ingroſſed, and ſent up to the lords.   So that important
" bill was never read but once in the houſe of commons, and was never
" committed; which, I believe, was never before heard of in parlia-
" ment [*q*]."

In order to aſcertain thoſe proceedings in the houſe of commons which
concluded in paſſing " A bill for the regulating of the privy-council,

[*q*] Hiſtory of the Rebellion, vol. i. p. 222.

" and

" and for taking away the court commonly called the ftar-chamber," we fhall ftate the material parts as they ftand in the journal.

1ma. *vice lecta eft billa.* " An act for declaring and regulating the power of the ftar-chamber and council-table."

1641. Mar. 26.

1ma. *vice lecta eft billa.* " An act for reforming of the unlawful acts and proceedings of the privy-council, and court, called the ftar-chamber."

30

2da. *vice lecta eft billa.* " An act for the reforming of the unlawful proceedings of the privy council, and court commonly called the ftar-chamber, upon queftion committed unto the committee for the ftar-chamber: and are to meet to morrow."

April 1ft.

2 . " *Ordered.* That the committee for the bill of the ftar-chamber " fhall have power to take the other bill concerning the ftar-chamber, " which has been once read, out of the houfe, and to take it into con- " fideration with the other bill, and out of both to make one, and pre- " fent it to the houfe."

" *Ordered.* That the bill of ftar-chamber, high commiffion court and " pluralities be reported on Thurfday morning next."

18

And after feveral fubfequent fimilar orders,

" Mr. *Prideaux* reports the bill concerning the ftar-chamber, and the " council-board, with the amendments: the which amendments were " twice read, and, upon queftion, ordered to be ingroffed [r]."

May 31ft

3^{tia}. *vice lecta billa.* " An act for the regulating the council table, and " taking away the court commonly called the ftar-chamber; and, upon " queftion, paffed."

June 8 *poft meridiem.*

" Mr. *Hampden* appointed to carry up thefe bills following to the " lords,"

9.

" An act for regulating the council table, and taking away the court commonly called the ftar-chamber."

" An act &c."

" Mr. *Prideaux* reports the bill of ftar-chamber returned from the lords at a conference by a felect committee of both houfes."

June 28. *p. meridm.*

[r] *Rufhworth* fays that on this day a bill for quite taking away the jurifdiction of the ftar-chamber was read.

" *Refolved,*

" *Refolved*, upon the queſtion, inſtead of the word, *henceforth*, ſhall be inſerted, *after the 1ſt. day of Auguſt*, in all three places."

" The amendments and additions and proviſoes, were all twice read, " and committed to Mr. *Selden*, Mr. *Prideaux*, Mr. *Maynard*, Sir *Tho.* " *Widdrington*, Mr. *Glyn*, Mr. *Hill*, Mr. *Perd*, Mr. *Cage*, Mr. *Rigby*, " Serjᵗ. *Wilde*, Sir *John Colpepper*, Mr. *Bagſhaw*, Mr. *Pierpoint*, Mr. " Mr. *Pelham*, Sir *Robᵗ. Harley*, and are to meet this afternoon at ſix of " the clock in the court of wards."

" Mr. *Prideaux* reports the bill concerning the council-board, and " ſtar chamber, returned from the lords at a conference, with ſome ad- " ditions, proviſoes, and alterations, the which were here read, and " afterwards committed."

" Reſolved, upon the queſtion, that theſe words, *in any other court* " *or courts whatſoever*, ſhall be preſented to the lords at a conference."

" In the 5th. addition, and in the 4th. line, after the word, *what-* " *ſoever*, that the clauſe there following may be omitted wholly, and " this clauſe added inſtead thereof, viz. *unleſs in ſuch cauſes where, by* " *the ſtatutes of this realm, they have power and authority to commit or* " *impriſon; and that in the warrant for ſuch commitment, impriſonment* " *or reſtraint the true cauſe thereof be ſo expreſſed, as the courts to which* " *the ſame ſhall be returned may well judge thereof*."

" The order made yeſterday for reſuming the conſideration of the " bills concerning the ſtar-chamber and high commiſſion was read."

" And the houſe accordingly proceeded with the amendments to theſe " bills returned from the lords and the Committee."

" The lords by meſſage deſire a preſent conference by a committee " of both houſes preſently in the painted chamber, if it may ſtand with " the convenience of this houſe, concerning the bill of the ſtar-cham- " ber,"

" Mr. *Prideaux* reports the amendments returned from the lords at " a ſecond conference to the bill concerning the ſtar-chamber and coun- " cil board."

* * * * * * * * * * * *

" Reſolved, upon the queſtion, That neither the body of the lords " of the council, nor any one of them in particular, as a privy coun-
ſellor,

" fellor, has any-power to imprison any free born subject, except in
" such cases as they are warranted by the statutes of the realm."

" Sir *John Hotham* went up with a message to the lords, to desire a
" free conference by a committee of the whole house presently, if it may
" stand with their conveniency, concerning the bill of star-chamber;
" and council-board. Brings answer that their lordships will give a
" present meeting by a committee of the whole house as is desired."

" The amendments, additions and provisoes to the bill concerning the
" star-chamber, now brought from the lords, were twice read, and upon
" question assented to; and the bill ordered to be amended accordingly.
" And, upon a second question, the provisoes were ordered to be in-
" grossed."

" The amendments, additions and provisoes to the bill concerning the
" high commission, now brought from the lords, were twice read, and,
" upon question assented unto; and the bill ordered to be amended
" accordingly. And upon a second question the provisoes were ordered
" to be ingrossed."

" 3^tia. *vice lecta.* The amendments and provisoes to the star-chamber
" bill were read in the ingrossed copy; and upon the question assented
" unto."

" 3^tia. *vice lecta.* The amendments and additions of the bill concern-
" ing the high commission were read, and upon question assented unto,
" and passed."

" A message from the lords by Mr. Attorney and Mr. Serj^t. *Finch.*"

" The lords command this message to be sent in writing (which was
" first read by Mr. attorney, and then delivered to Mr. speaker, *in hæc*
" *verba*) *The king hath been moved upon the desire of both houses by some*
" *lords for his royal assent unto the three bills sent up this morning. That*
" *his majesty will come this morning, and give his royal assent unto the bill*
" *which concerns raising of monies for disbanding the armies, for the present*
" *ease of the kingdom: that in regard his majesty hath not been acquainted*
" *with the particulars of the other two bills he will advise of them until*
" *Tuesday next; and then will give his answer.*"

" Lord *Falkland* is appointed to go to the lords with this message."

" To

" To acquaint their lordfhips that this houfe has taken into confide-
" ration their lordfhips meffage ; and do conceive that the paffing of the
" two bills concerning the ftar-chamber and high commiffion, will . . . .
" much expedition to the levying of monies appointed to be raifed by
" the act for raifing of monies for difbanding the armies &c. and there-
" fore to defire their lordfhips that his majefty may be moved to give the
" royal affent to them all three together with all convenient fpeed."

On the 5th his majefty gave the royal affent to thefe two bills.

In order to complete the hiftory of the proceedings in the houfe of
commons relative to the court of ftar-chamber, I fhall here fet forth the
following particulars not inferted in their proper place.

" November 7th. [1640] The firft petition which was preferred and
" read in the houfe, was that of *Sufannah Baftwick* ; and afterwards,
" another of *Sarah Burton*, on the behalf of their refpective hufbands,
" clofe prifoners in remote iflands ; complaining of the fevere fentence
" of the court of ftar-chamber, inflicted upon them in the pillory ; and
" that the petitioners, their wives, were by particular order not to be
" permitted to come and vifit their hufbands.   Whereupon the houfe or-
" dered, *That their faid hufbands fhall be forthwith fent for to the parlia-*
" *ment, in fafe cuftody, by warrant of this houfe, directed to the governors*
" *of the ifles where they are prifoners, and to the captains of the caftles*
" *there ; and that the caufe of their detainer may be certified hither*
" *alfo.*"

" The next petition preferred was that of *John Brown*, a fervant to
" Mr. *Prynn*, clofe prifoner in the ifle of *Jerfey*, complaining of the
" fentence in the ftar-chamber againft his mafter, and the cruel putting
" it in execution ; and of his banifhment to a remote ifland ; defiring the
" houfe would fend for his mafter, more fully to make known his cafe :
" and the houfe made the like order for him as was made for Dr.
" *Baftwick* [*s*]."

From what preceeds it is evident that the houfe of commons had under
their confideration the legal and affumed jurifdiction of the court of ftar-

[*s*] *Rufhworth*, vol. iv. p. 20.

chamber,

chamber, with its great and manifold abufes, from the 7th. of November 1640, to the begining of July following, during which time, by themfelves and their various committees, one of which, without fpeaking of the reft, was compofed, with other perfons, of men whofe confummate learning and profound knowledge of law and government, with other abilities, have been feldom equalled in this or any other kingdom, they received the petitions of the parties aggrieved, gave proper orders for their liberation, and every thing requifite for the fupport of their petitions, confidered the certificates of their imprifonment, with their caufes, heard the petitioners in perfon, or by counfel, examined their witneffes and papers, and infpected the records of the enormous proceedings and decrees of this court, making the moft diligent and ftrict enquiry into the verity and nature of all thofe facts which upon full confideration were with great reafon held to be the proper grounds of its diffolution; and in their proceeding by bill to declare and regulate the power of the ftar-chamber and council-table, and by another bill to reform their unlawful acts and proceedings; and by a third, formed of them, which in its progrefs was rendered effectual, for regulating the privy council, and taking away the court of ftar-chamber, governing themfelves with great deliberation and advifement; and in proper feafon conferring from time to time with the lords, whereby they united their wifdom with their own; fo that, notwithstanding lord *Clarendons* reprefentation, this law was no precipitate act of the ftate, or of the houfe of commons in particular, but the fruit of a patient hearing of all proper parties, a careful examination, mature confideration, and confequent knowledge of all its fubject matters, and neceffary to the reftoration of legal liberty and equal juftice, the chief ends of all good government.

An intelligent friend informs me that the records and papers which belonged to this court are no where to be found, being deftroyed, as he fuppofes, to prevent their proving to pofterity the particulars of all thofe grievances which thefe judges impofed on their fellow fubjects, under colour and in the name of public juftice, founding their decrees on their paffions, their arbitrary wills, foreign laws, *civil* or *canon*, or on any thing rather than the proper principles of law, equity, or humanity; and

whofe

whofe cruelty feems to have wanted nothing to complete it but the power and ufe of torture, the ufual companion of the *civil* law.

On repeated enquiry, I have to my furprize found that the rack or brake, brought into the tower by the duke of *Exeter* for a beginning of the *civil* laws, intended to be introduced by him, the duke of *Suffolk*, and others, is ftill remaining there : and upon confidering that fo long as the kingdom endures innocent perfons will be liable to imprifonment there, thro' the appearance of guilt, the confpiracy of others, or their public virtue exerted for the advancement of the common-weal, or to preferve it from the dictates of bold ambition, the baneful influence or mifconduct of minifters unequal to their places, or to punifh and extirpate peculation and corruption, that fell deftroyer of free ftates, for which, though more dangerous than the fword of our enemies, numerous advocates have with fo great effrontery contended, which minifters have in times paft with impunity practiced, and which being promoted by thofe who ought as far as poffible to prevent it, by its diffufion, polutes the land with bribery, perjury, fraud, drunkennefs and idlenefs, thereby fapping the foundation of the ftate, as the great political architects in all ages have, for our warning, with united voice declared—that the more thefe men of noble minds are wanted, the more danger will attend the vigorous exercife of their virtues ; and when in confequence thereof they find themfelves confined in the fame place with that horrid inftrument of torture to which the innocent have been fo often fubjected, this may occafion fuch apprehenfions as every fincere lover of liberty and juftice would willingly prevent—that the mildnefs and excellence of the *Englifh* conftitution and government have augmented the ftate in numbers, wealth and ftrength, and given to its members that fpirit which renders them invincible.   Sir *Thomas Smith,* after applauding the magnanimity of the *Englifh* nation, and cenfuring the torment or queftion ufed by order of the *civil* law, and cuftom of other countries, as incompatible with it, fays. " The nature of our nation is free, ftout of heart, prodigal of life " and bloud : but contumely, beating, fervitude, and fervile torment and " punifhment it will not abide. So in this nature and fafhion our an- " cient princes and *legiflators* have nourifhed them as to make them ftout-
" hearted

" hearted, couragious, and foldiers, not villains and flaves; and that is
" the fcope almoft of all our policy [*t*]."—that the defign formed by the
duke of *Exeter*, and duke of *Suffolk*, the queens great favorite, and
others, of introducing the *civil* laws, with the actual bringing in of the
rack for a beginning, by the completion whereof the *Englifh* government
would have been changed, and its dignity diminifhed, the freedom of the
people fubverted, and their bodies fubjected to dire tortures, was apparently, in my opinion, treafon againft the common-wealth; and yet thefe
great offenders, who thus confpired to take away the common right, and
beft inheritance of all their follow fubjects; and fupplanting the law of
liberty, equity, fafety, and mercy, to debafe and enflave the whole kingdom, were fuffered to go unqueftioned, inftead of being duely punifhed
for this atrocious crime—that the reign of a mild prince being the proper
feafon for deftroying every inftrument of intended public cruelty, under
favour, and a firm perfuafion that this, which was placed in the tower,
in order to be employed as the mean of inflicting fuch excruciating torments upon the *Englifh* fubjects, is abhorrent to his majeftys humane difpofition, as well as odious to his people, I would humbly fubmit to proper
confideration that this horrid inftrument, inftead of continuing an object
of terror in the capital prifon of a free country, be publicly burned, in
honour to the mildnefs of his majeftys government, and the freedom of
his fubjects from all torture.

Our enquiry into the nature, proceedings, and abolition of the court of
ftar-chamber hath, I prefume, clearly fhewn that the refolutions of that
court, which were intended to form, and have been fuppofed to contain
a complete body of laws touching libels, are void of all proper authority,
fo that they cannot be enforced on the fubject as law in any fenfe whatever, yet I cannot forbear faying that it hath ever appeared ftrange to me
that lawyers bred up in the regular ftudy and knowledge of the great and
fundamental laws of the land, and in juft admiration of their wifdom
and equity, and of thofe impartial and judicious explications which,
confonant to their fpirit and intent, the fages of the law have made for

[*t*] Common-wealth of *England*, B. ii. ch. 27.

the

the public utility, in thofe times wherein the ftreams of juftice flowed free and pure, being unpolluted and unreftrained by the hand of power, fhould through inadvertence acknowledge, or with follicitude contend for, the decifions given in the ftar-chamber by a collection of courtiers devoted to the pleafure of princes of arbitrary difpofitions as good authorities, and in effect laws, at this day. And, in order to prove that the arbitrary meafures of king *James*, fupported by his council, who under different appellations ferved him for the purpofes of advice and enforcement thereof, were advanced to a dangerous excefs before thofe refolutions were formed in the great cafe of L. P. whofe authority I oppofe, I defire that, befides the other matters before mentioned, it may be particularly remembered that thefe refolutions were made in *Eafter* term, in the third year of the reign of king *James*, and that on the 17th. day of October preceding the proclamation or letters patent afore-mentioned were iffued refpecting tobacco imported, by which the king affumed the power of impofing what duties he pleafed, of fubjecting the goods of the merchants to forfeiture, and them to fuch pecuniary penalties, and corporal punifhments as their high offence in not conforming to his command fhould deferve; thereby fubjecting the merchants to fuch exceffive fines as the court of ftar-chamber fhould in their difcretion think fit; and moreover to fuch various, indignant and cruel corporal punifhments as that court fhould from time to time in their wonted feveriry be enclined to inflict. For my own part I know no language equal to the malignity of this proceeding of king *James*, who by this fingle act of defpotifm violated the rights of his fubjects in their goods, monies, and bodies, fubjecting thofe refpectable and ufeful men the merchants of *England*, on their difobedience to his lawlefs commands, to fuch ignominious punifhments as are unfit to be mentioned with their names, hereby manifefting his injurious notions refpecting his monarchic authority, his luft of unlimited power, and the contempt and difhonour in which he held the rights, liberties, and people of this kingdom.

Notwithftanding that upon due examination it appears that the two ftar-chamber cafes fo often referred to long fince loft their authority, I fhall proceed to confider the matter contained in them fo far as relates

to

to the principal propofition, after taking notice of the two cafes mentioned by lord *Coke*, which happened in the reign of *Edward* III. The record or report of the former is imperfect, and therefore it would not ferve for a proper foundation whereon to reft an enquiry into the nature of libels againft private perfons, in cafe that was my prefent purpofe: but, after bearing my feeble teftimony againft thofe who proftitute their pens, or the prefs to promote their injurious defigns, I defire it may be remembered that my concern is not with contefts between private perfons, or their confequent treatment of each other, the amount of that general propofition which I would fupport as beneficial to the public being only this, " That matters of public concernment are the proper " objects of public knowledge." There is a great and manifeft difference between thefe and the other in their nature, relations and confequences. Upon the cafe of *John de Northampton* it may be obferved, (1) that being an attorney of the court of king's bench, he ftood in a fpecial relation to the judges; and as all duties are the confequents of the relations of the parties, they feem to have confidered him as having acted an improper part, inconfiftent with his duty to them, and to have proceeded againft him accordingly. 2. The matter charged upon him, I apprehend, was infufficient to conftitute a crime in any common perfon. He did not charge the juftices with having done any thing illegal, or improper; but faid, that neither the chief juftice, nor his fellows, would do any great thing by the command of the king or queen more than of any other of the realm. By the oath of the juftices made in the fame year wherein this proceeding was had, it was, among other things, provided that they fhould well and lawfully ferve their lord the king, and his people, in the office of juftice, and do equal law and execution of right to all his fubjects rich and poor, without having regard to any perfon, to the kings letters, or any other mans, or to any other caufe. And the words of this attorney might, I conceive, have been confidered as matter of undefigned commendation rather than cenfure of the judges, who being properly left to the free exercife of their judgment, it ought to be prefumed that they would fully and freely difcharge their duty to the king and his people in every point, upon which no great thing could remain to be done in virtue of the kings command, in its nature im-

proper

proper as well as needlefs.   3. By the judgment of the court it was declared, firft, that the letter contained no truth, that is, in effect, faying that they would do a great thing by the kings command. Secondly, that this letter might caufe the kings indignation to arife againft the court and his juftices, which would be to their fcandal.   Now, with all due reverence to the memory of thefe learned judges, in my humble opinion, it would have been more for the honour of this magnanimous prince, under whom the kingdom fo greatly flourifhed in laws and arms, to have prefumed that his indignation was not to be incited againft this honourable court by this general, idle, and impertinent letter; written by a forward, conceited, and petulant attorney practifing in it; and thefe fears of poffible royal refentment appear to be but a weak foundation of a judgment given for committing a fubject to prifon : however, thefe judges being ftrangers to the ftar-chamber feverities, they probably foon difcharged him, upon giving fureties for his good behaviour.

And now we fhall in courfe confider thofe refolutions of the court of ftar-chamber which contravene a free enquiry into public affairs; and all bufineffes being what thofe who manage them make them, this enquiry of neceffity comprifes the managers with the matters. The chief of thefe refolutions is the fourth in number in the firft cafe, and is thus expreffed. " It is not material whether the libel be true, or whether the party " againft whom it is made be of good or ill fame."   Thefe words, I apprehend, contain fuch a profcription of truth, and the provifion of fuch a fanctuary for weak and wicked men, who, through the unhappy miftakes of princes, the power and prejudice of minifters, or the combination, or other influence of the Great, who fometimes fcruple not to make their country a convenience to themfelves, their adherents and dependents, fuftain public offices, as are inconfiftent with the juft liberty and fafety of a free people, and would in effect, under fome princes, fix an indelible character on their unqualified minifters and their partifans. But we fhall proceed to the examination of the reafon affigned for this twofold refolution, to wit, " for in a fettled ftate of government the " party grieved ought to complain for every injury done him in an or- " dinary courfe of law, and not by any means to revenge himfelf, either " by the odious courfe of libelling, or otherwife."   This propofed equi-
                                                                            valent

valent of the pen and the prefs will by no means fupply their place; they are profitably employed upon the nature and foundation of human government, the exellence and defects of their various forms, the particular conftitution of the ftate of which the author is a member, with the means of its perfection and prefervation; and in monarchies limited and tempered by laws, in giving their beft affiftance for clearly diftinguifhing and preferving the juft boundaries between the princes prerogative and the peoples liberty, both being neceffary to the common good; in the examination and reprefentation of the nature and condition of the feveral parts of an extended empire, and their mutual interefts and relations, with the relations of the whole to other ftates; in confidering the wifdom, propriety, and utility of laws, or their defects through miftakes in their formation, or the mutabiliy of human affairs; and, as the prefervation of a free ftate greatly depends on the manners and cuftoms of its members, in pointing out to thofe who are willing to fave their country, and blefs their pofterity, fuch manners and cuftoms as are beneficial or prejudicial to their fafety and lafting happinefs; in preventing the abufes of authority or liberty, fo that the former may not run into power and tyranny, or the latter into licentioufnefs; and in promoting the knowledge of truth, the common friend of all, with every thing that may tend to the advancement of the common weal; and, after examining, with freedom, propriety, and care, public meafures, and the merits or demerits of public perfons, bringing all to the proper teft, that perpetual law, which being made in heaven cannot be repealed on earth, Salus populi suprema lex esto.

The ftar-chamber reafon for their refolution hath no relation to the ufe of writing in thefe or any fimilar cafes, which differ fo widely from thofe perfonal injuries that may be redreffed by known ftanding laws in the eftablifhed courts of juftice. And, in fupport of the claim made to the free ufe of writing upon public affairs, I fhall endeavour to evince its farther util ty, by confidering the conduct of fome of thofe princes who reftrained it, with the benefits that might have refulted from its permiffion. The moft glorious empire had by numerous conquefts been formed and extended from *Rome* by its policy and arms, the feveral parts being gradually and firmly connected with each other, and with the mother
city,

city, the center of the whole, and the heart of this great body politic : but *Conſtantine* , moved by the vanity of being the founder of a new city, broke up that noble and compact political ſtructure, which wiſdom accompanying the the extenſion of the empire had formed, and time had improved, ſtrengthened, and rendered moſt convenient, by his removal of the ſeat of empire to *Byzantium*, which he adorned with the ſpoils of many cities. After this he made bare the principal borders of the empire, drawing off the legions, and placing them in the provinces, where they became effeminate. Now let us ſuppoſe that ſundry perſons poſſeſſed of the true *Roman* ſpirit, had in virtue of the liberty of writing freely, in language equal to ſo great occaſions, challenged his attention, expoſed his policy, and, in effect, roundly told him that by his intended diviſion of the capital, and the removal of the ſeat of power to ſo great a diſtance from the more warlike nations, it would become impracticable to collect and diſtribute the forces of the empire for its beſt protection; whereby the whole would be weakened, and *Rome*, the miſtreſs of the world, not only diſhonoured, but in time brought into danger of falling into the arms of barbarians—that inſtead of a body politic, revered by all nations for its grandeur and excellence, he was going to form a double-headed monſter, and that truth being mighty above all things, poſterity would conſider him as the deſtroyer of the moſt renowned empire, rather than the founder of a city ; this plain dealing, notwithſtanding the wonted violence of mean ambition, might poſſibly have checked this emperour in the career of his vanity, and inciting wiſer counſels prevented his miſpending his time and his treaſure upon this vain-glorious and injurious project. And afterwards in ſtrong terms declaring that by his departure from the former wiſe policy, in drawing away the legions from the banks of the great rivers, and diſtributing them in the provinces, the empire would be laid open to the incurſions of barbarians, and the ſoldiers, who were its defence, enervated by the pleaſures of the circus and the theatre, whereby the ſtate would be ſtill farther weakened and endangered, this might have occaſioned better conſideration, and contributed to ſecure the borders. And again, when the partiality and perſonal regard of this emperour for his favorites were ſuch that he gave them too great authority, and, though he knew their in-
juſtice,

juftice, could not prevail upon himfelf to punifh them, if he had been told that by this proceeding he facrificed his own honour, and the welfare of his fubjeĉts to the fupport of men, who, inftead of being favoured with his proteĉtion, ought to feel the weight of his indignation, and that he who does not reftrain the known injuries of his fervants does in effeĉt commit them, this might have caufed a change in his conduĉt, and prevented fo deep a ftain from being for ever fixed on that charaĉter which he was fo folicitous to raife and preferve. Though furnamed the *Great*, this proceeding was inconfiftent with all true grandeur, and clearly fhewed that the reafon by him affigned for his fecond and fourth ediĉts againft libels was illufory and vain, to wit, that the writers of what he deemed libels fhould openly accufe the perfons mentioned in them.

The ediĉt of *Theodofius* the *Great*, fo full of dignity, clemency and favourable regard for the freedom of fpeech and writing, with the equitable conduĉt which at length took place of indignant wrath, may attone in fome meafure for his intended fevere treatment of the city of *Antioch*; but in cafe he had fome years before publifhed this ediĉt, through the indulgence therein contained, he might have been told that it was effential to juftice that punifhments fhould be proportionate to offences—that the offence committed by a part of the inhabitants, in cafting down the ftatues of the emprefs, could by no means warrant the deftruĉtion of the firft city in the world, with the diftrefs, and difperfion of all perfons remaining in it, after many who were innocent had fuffered death together with the guilty in expiation of this offence.—That the regal law under which the emperours claimed all the authority and power of the people, as containing their conceffion thereof, could never be intended for the deftruĉtion, but for the prefervation of cities, and that if he executed his purpofe, inftead of being confidered as a great and good prince, all ages and nations would feverely cenfure this cruel proceeding. Thefe interefting and plain truths might have roufed the dormant humanity of this emperour, and fo prevented this great city from continuing fo long under the terrible apprehenfions of utter extirpation; and moreover they might poffibly have prevented that horrid cruelty which he exercifed an another occafion. The inhabitants of *Theffalonica* having in a fedition flain one of his lieutenant generals, he abandoned the whole city to the mercy of

his

his foldiers, who flew fifteen thoufand perfons before they were fated
with blood, involving the innocent in the fame condition with the
guilty.

The moft learned perfons differing in their opinions touching the motives that induced *Theodofius* to publifh this remarkable edict, I defire leave
to mention my own conjecture, that he was in fome meafure influenced
herein by the oration of *Latinus Pacatus*. This orator being fent from
Gaul to *Rome*, to congratulate *Theodofius* upon his victory obtained over
the tyrant *Maximus*, on the firft of September, in the year 39:, according to the account of the beft chronologers, he pronounced his oration,
addreffed to the emperour in the fenate; when, after faying many things,
he fpake thus.

" Who could compare himfelf to us in calamity? We fuftained the
" tyrant alone, and in conjunction with others. Not to mention the
" utter defolation of cities, defarts filled with fugitive nobles, or the con-
" fifcation of the effects of perfons who had fuftained the higheft hon-
" ours, themfelves put on a level with the vulgar, and a price fet on
" their heads, we have feen dignities debafed, men of confular dignity
" defpoiled of their robes, old men furviving their fortunes, and the la-
" mentable fecurity of infants fporting even under the fequeftrator,
" while at the fame time though miferable we were forbid to appear
" wretched, yea we were even compelled to feign ourfelves happy;
" and having at home, and in fecret, entrufted to our wives and children
" alone the furtive grief, we went abroad with a countenance not fuiting
" our fortune. For you would hear an informer fay, why does that man
" appear fad? Is it becaufe he is reduced from riches to poverty? Why
" is he not thankful that he lives? Why appears this man abroad in
" mourning? He laments, I fuppofe, a brother; but he hath a fon.
" Thus we were not permitted to bewail what was loft, through fear of
" what remained. We therefore veiled our cloudy minds with ferene
" countenances, and, like thofe who having tafted the juice of *Sardoan*
" grafs are faid to fmile in death, when over-whelmed with forrow we
" perfonated the chearful. It is fome alleviation of calamities to give
" tears to our evils, and to relax the breaft with fighs. There is no
" greater punifhment than to be miferable without being fuffered to ap-
                                                    " pear

" pear so. At the same time there was no hope of satisfying the spoiler ;
" for satiety did not, as is natural, follow abundance, the eager desire of
" having daily encreased, and what was procured did but irritate the
" rage of obtaining. As drink encreaseth the thirst of sick persons ; as
" fire is not smothered but encreased by dry fuel ; so the riches accu-
" mulated by the public impoverishment, served only to stimulate the
" greediness of the hungry mind [*u*]."

And now taking leave of the *Romans*, and coming to *England*, the notoriety of the times wherein the free and proper use of writing upon
public affairs might have been beneficial to prince and people, who can
have no true separate interests, will in a great measure render these particular examinations unnecessary, which, by reason of their nature and
number, would at present be impracticable ; nevertheless it may briefly
be observed that in the reigns of *Henry* VI. and *Edward* IV. reproachful
words, idle prophecies, calculates of nativity, rhimes and ballads, spoken
and made of the king, were prosecuted and punished as treason ; and in
the beginning of the reign of this latter prince the law of treason was
so far extended that one *Walter Walker*, a citizen and grocer of *London*,
was executed in *Smithfield* as a traitor, for having said that he would
make his son heir to the crown, meaning the sign of the crown in *Cheap-*

[*u*] § 25. Quis se nobis calamitate contulerit ? Tyrannum & cum aliis tulimus, & soli.
Quid ergo referam vacuatas municipibus suis civitates, impletas fugitivis nobilibus solitudines ?
Quid perfunctorum honoribus summis virorum bona publicata, capita diminuta, vitam ære tax-
ata ? Vidimus redactas in numerum dignitates, & exutos trabeis consulares, & senes fortuna-
rum superstites, & infantium sub ipso sectore ludentium flendam securitatem ; cum interim
miseri vetabamur agere miseros ; imo etiam cogebamur mentiri beatos ; & cum domi atque secreto
solis conjugibus ac liberis credidissemus furtivum dolorem, procedebamus in publicum non nostræ
fortunæ vultu. Audires enim dicere delatorem. Quid ita ille tristis incedit ? An quia pauper
ex divite est ? Non enim se vivere gratulatur ? Quid ita hic publicum atratus incestat ? Luget,
credo, fratrem. Sed habet filium. Ita fleri non licebat amissa, metu reliquorum. Serenos
ergo nubilis mentibus vultus induebamus, &, ad illorum vicem qui degustato Sardorum gramine
succo feruntur in morte ridere, imitabamur læta mœrentes. Est aliquod calamitatum delini-
mentum dedisse lacrymas malis, & pectus laxasse suspiriis. Nulla major est pœna quam esse
miserum, nec videri. Spes inter hæc nulla prædonis explendi. Nec enim, ut natura fert,
copiam satietas sequebatur, crescebat indies habendi fames, & parandi rabiem parta irritabant.
Ut ægrorum sitim potus accendit, ut ignis arentibus non obruitur, sed augetur, ita coactæ
publica egestate divitiæ aviditatem jejunæ mentis acuebant.

side.

fide. This putting of an innocent man to death for a meer jeft was an act of tyranny, accompanied with fuch proftitution of public juftice as greatly difhonoured the jurifprudence of the kingdom. And although I would by no means attempt to juftifie or excufe opprobrious or indecent words fpoken or written of the king, in profe or verfe; yet I am wholly unable to reconcile the various profecutions and punifhments for the other offences, which took place in the reign of *Henry* VI. with the law of the land, or with that impunity which was vouchfafed to the dukes of *Exeter* and *Suffolk*, and others, with refpect to their atrocious crime in bringing in the rack for a beginning of the *civil* laws. All bodies politic, as well as natural, are indued with the principle of felf-prefervation, and this principle, I prefume, is inherent in every individual confidered in his focial as well as natural ftate; and therefore I conceive that every man when he found that thefe audacious offenders, encouraged by the affurance of that royal favour which they abufed, had actually begun their intended fubverfion of the common laws and liberties of the kingdom, which were fo well fuited to the genius and difpofition of its inhabitants, through the enjoyment whereof it had fo greatly flourifhed; and that, inftead of the former fafety touching his life, limbs, and eftate, the whole was now to be fubjected to a new regimen, and to unknown difficulties, diftrefs and danger, had good reafon, in order to his prefervation in common with others, by words or writing to cenfure the injurious proceeding and defigns of thefe public perfons, and make every fuch reprefentation of the nature and confequences thereof as might tend to obviate this impending calamity; and it is poffible that a full, clear and decent reprefentation of the great unfitnefs and danger of thofe councils, connections and dependances that took place in this princes court might have alarmed the chief parties, and prevented the tragical effects of the conduct of an imperious intriguing queen, who by her infidious arts having obtained the fole command, after deftroying the kings friends, governing by her paffions, embroiled the whole kingdom, in confequence whereof the king loft his liberty and his life, being the laft prince of the houfe of *Lancafter*, which had made the greateft figure in *Europe*.

The

The avarice of *Henry* VII. was so insatiate, that, if the star-chamber court had not existed, and writing freely had been allowed, the ablest pens, I conceive, could not have checked it ; for having obtained the unjust and injurious act aforecited, by force whereof *Empson* and *Dudley*, and such justices of peace (corrupt men) as they caused to be authorized, during so many years, committed most grievous and heavy exactions and oppressions, he continued to receive the fruit of the whole, by these and other like oppressions and injustice collecting vast treasures ; so that lord *Coke*, in his chapter of Wards and Liveries, says, " by the close roll in " anno 3 *Hen.* VIII. it appeareth that the king left in his coffers fifty " and three hundred thousand pounds, most part in foreign coin, which " in those days was not of least value." *Qui facit per alterum facit per se*; and these oppressions being committed and enforced in the name, by the authority, and to the use of the king, he was the oppressor: but although greedy avarice, supported by an unjust law, was regardless of these grievances; yet a true and proper public representation of the state of the distressed, with a thorough examination into the nature of that injurious act, which was the source of their sufferings, might have occasioned such a just and general consideration of the whole matter as in its consequences would have caused a repeal of this act by the parliament in being, or on failure thereof have influenced the kingdom to chuse such representatives as having better knowledge and greater regard for fundamental laws, natural justice and equity, and being animated with true public spirit, would have examined with diligence into these manifold grievances, and frustrating and avoiding all the arts, influence and management of this subtle prince and his agents, would have prevented this oppressive act from continuing in force til after his death.

Constantine the *Great* by his failing to punish the injustice of those to whom he gave too great authority has to this day suffered in his memory, although it was never suggested that he availed himself in the least measure of their misdeeds, where as the greatest genious, being more inclined to adulation and palliation than to a strict observance of truth, the soul of history, hath bestowed upon *Henry* great and unworthy commendation. This historian speaking of the parliament held in the third year of this kings reign, says that according to the lord chancellors admonition there
were

were that parliament divers excellent laws ordained concerning the points which the king recommended; firſt the authority of the ſtar chamber which before ſubſiſted by the ancient common laws of the realm, was confirmed in certain caſes; and after relating the particulars of the ſuffering of Sir *William Stanley*, who had ſaved the kings life, and ſet the crown upon his head, he writes thus, " the fall of this great man, being " in ſo high authority and favour (as was thought) with the king; and " the manner of carriage of the buſineſs, as if there had been ſecret " inquiſition upon him for a great time before; and the cauſe for which " he ſuffered, which was little more than for ſaying in effect, that the " title of *York* was better than the title of *Lancaſter*, which was the caſe " almoſt of every man (at the leaſt in opinion) was matter of great terror " amongſt all the kings ſervants and ſubjects; inſomuch as no man almoſt " thought himſelf ſecure, and men durſt ſcarce commune or talk one " with another, but there was a general diffidence every where: which " neverthelefs made the king rather more abſolute than more ſafe. For " bleeding inwards, and ſhut vapours, ſtrangle ſooneſt, and oppreſs moſt."

" Hereupon preſently came forth ſwarms and volies of libels (which " are the guſts of liberty of ſpeech reſtrained, and the females of ſedi- " tion) containing bitter invectives and ſlanders againſt the king, and " ſome of the council: for the contriving and diſperſing whereof (after " great diligence of enquiry) five mean perſons were caught up and " executed." And coming to the twenty third year of his reign he writes as follows, " And hearing alſo of the bitter cries of his people " againſt the oppreſſions of *Dudley* and *Empſon*, and their complices, " partly by devout perſons about him, and partly by public ſermons " (the preachers doing their duty therein) he was touched with great " remorſe for the ſame. Neverthelefs *Empſon* and *Dudley*, though they " could not but hear of theſe ſcruples in the kings conſcience; yet, as " if the kings ſoul and his money were in ſeveral offices, that the one " was not to intermeddle with the other, went on with as great rage " as ever. For the ſame 23d. year was there a ſharp proſecution againſt " Sir *William Capel* now the ſecond time; and this was for matters of " miſgovernment in his mayoralty; the great matter being that in ſome " payments he had taken knowledge of falſe monies, and did not his " diligence

" diligence to examine and beat it out who were the offenders.　For this
" and some other things laid to his charge he was condemned to pay
" £ 2000; and being a man of stomach, and hardened by his former
" troubles, refused to pay a mite, and belike used some untoward speeches
" of the proceedings, for which he was sent to the tower, and there
" remained til the kings death.　*Knesworth* likewise, that had been
" lately mayor of *London*, and both his sheriffs, were for abuses in their
" offices questioned, and imprisoned, and delivered, upon £ 1000 paid.
" *Hawis*, an Alderman of *London*, was put in trouble, and died with
" thought and anguish, before his business came to an end.　Sir *Lawrence*
" *Ailmer*, who had likewise been mayor of *London*, and his two sheriffs,
" were put to the fine of £ 1000.　And Sir *Lawrence* for refusing to make
" payment, was committed to prison, where he stayed til *Empson* himself
" was committed in his place."

Nevertheless he begins this princes character in these words.　" This
" king (to speak of him in terms equal to his deserving) was one of the
" best sort of wonders; a wonder for wise men.　He had parts both in his
" virtues and his fortune not so fit for a common place, as for observa-
" tion.　Certainly he was religious, both in his affection and obser-
" vance."

The state prosecutions and punishments in this reign, and in the reigns
of *Henry* VI. and *Edward* IV. wherein writings and words criminal,
and even innocent, were perverted or aggravated and inhansed into treason,
and matters were brought to such a pass, that, using the words of king
Henry IV. to his first parliament, it may be said, that " no man knew,
" as he ought to know, how to do, speak, or say, for doubt of the pains
" of treason," shew the necessity of adhering to a certain boundary of this
great crime, and " how dangerous it is by construction and analogy to
" make treasons where the law [25 Edward III.] has not done it ; for
" such a method admits of no limits or bounds, but runs as far as the
" wit and invention of accusers, and the odiousness and detestation of
" persons accused will carry men [w]."

Notwithstanding the notoriety of that great love that king *Henry* VIII.
had of power and profusion, the parliament which he convened in the

[w] *Hales* pleas of the Crown, Part I. Ch. 11.

thirty-

thirty-firſt year of his reign were ſo devoted to his will that they paſſed an act in theſe words.

" The king for the time being, with the advice of his council, or the " more part of them, may ſet forth proclamations under ſuch penalties " and pains as to him and them ſhall ſeem neceſſary, which ſhall be " obſerved as though they were made by act of parliament; but this " ſhall not be prejudicial to any perſons inheritance, offices, liberties, " goods, chattels, or life; and whoſoever ſhall willingly offend any " article contained in the ſaid proclamation, ſhall pay ſuch forfeitures, " or be ſo long impriſoned as ſhall be expreſſed in the ſaid proclamation; " and if any offending will depart the realm, to the intent he will not " anſwer his ſaid offence, he ſhall be adjudged a traitor."

Certain words [x] ſpoken or written of the king had ſome years before been made treaſon; but by this act he was enabled, with the advice of the more part of his council, to create new offences, in word writing or deed, at his pleaſure. The grant of ſo large a portion of deſpotic power to the king was ſo great and manifeſt a breach of the conſtitution of the kingdom, made by thoſe who were under the higheſt obligations to do their utmoſt to preſerve it, as would fully prove, if it were wanted, the fallibility of parliaments, and the utility of writing freely for their ſakes, or rather for the ſake of their conſtituents, for whoſe uſe they have their political exiſtence, without having recourſe to the unconſtitutional, dangerous, and injurious acts paſſed in the reign of *Henry* VII; and what was objected by ſome public ſpirited perſons in *Scotland* to thoſe acts which aſcribed to their king ſuch exorbitant powers, to wit, that they were " obtained from parliaments by the too great influence " of their monarchs, and the too great puſillanimity of parliaments, who " could not reſign the rights and privileges of the people, ſince they have " no warrant from them for that effect," might well have been objected to the act which gave the force of laws to the proclamations of the king for the time being.

Coming to the reign of queen *Mary*, let us obſerve that the *Romiſh* clergy, when poſſeſſed of that plentitude of power which is ever the

[x] To wit, heretic, ſchiſmatic, infidel, or uſurper of the Crown.

chief

chief object of their desire, have exercised their tyranny without any other bounds or remission than such as might serve to continue or to restore and strengthen it. *Pasce oves* meant *rege mundum*; and their arts and seductions being equal to their manifold oppressions, tyranizing over the minds, and consequently over the bodies and estates of men, to raise their supreme dominant state they subjected all princes, potentates, states and persons in christendom, and to preserve and enforce their power and their laws they maintained under reverend names innumerable troops at the expense of the princes whom they governed, and the people whom they enslaved; the regulars being the popes standing forces, and the seculars his militia, the former being computed to amount to two millions at least; the cruelties practised by *Christian* princes acting under their influence being chargeable on them, who prostituted the best religion to the worst purposes, and who improving in subtilty and severity, when the voice of truth was heard complaining of these grievances, to secure their tyranny, and silence her, whose invincible arguments, if heard, would overthrow it, devised a new species of cruelty, the prohibition of publishing books without their license. The use of these fetters on the mind, with its noble productions, was adopted by the court of star-chamber, and afterwards by the second, long, or pensionary parliament of king *Charles* II, who by their act passed in the fourteenth year of his reign [*y*], after prohibiting the printing of any heretical, seditious, schismatical or offensive books or pamphlets, &c. provided that no private persons should print, or cause to be printed, any book or pamphlet, unless the same were first licensed according to the directions therein contained, and that the kings messengers by warrant under his majestys sign manual, or under the hand of one or more of his principal secretaries of state, should have power, with a constable, to take such assistance as they should think needful, and at what time they should think fit to search all houses and shops where they should know, or on probable reason suspect, any books or papers to be printed, bound or stitched, especially printing houses, &c. to view what was there printing &c. and to examine whether the same were licensed &c. with power to seize books imprint-

[*y*] Cap. 33.

ing

ing without licenfe, together with the offenders, and to carry them before one or more juftices of the peace, to be by them committed to prifon, there to remain until tried and acquited, or convicted and punifhed; and alfo provided that in cafe thefe fearchers fhould find any books un-licenfed which they fufpected to contain matters contrary to the doctrine or difcipline of the church of *England*, or againft the ftate and govern-ment, they fhould feize upon fuch books, and carry them to the arch-bifhop of *Canterbury* or bifhop of *London*, or to one of the fecretaries of ftate, who fhould take fuch further courfe for their fuppreffion as to them fhould feem fit; fubjecting all printers &c. for the firft offence to the difability of exercifing their trades for three years, and for the fecond offence to perpetual difability, with fuch further punifhment by fine, imprifonment, or other corporal punifhment, not extending to life or limb, as the juftices of the court of kings bench, of oyer and terminer, or of affize, or juftices of the peace in their quarter feffions, fhould think fit to inflict. This act was made to continue in force two years; and by fubfequent acts paffed in the fixteenth, and in the fixteenth and feventeenth years of this kings reign, it was continued from time to time, and in the feventeenth year it was continued to the end of the firft feffion of the next parliament; fo that it expired in the month of May 1679; and by an act paffed in the firft year of the reign of king *James* II it was revived, and continued for the fpace of feven years from the 24th. of June 1685.

By this law it is evident the makers of it grafted on the papal ftock feveral fevere regulations and penalties nearly affecting the fubjects in their habitations, trades, monies, liberties and bodies, devifed by the court or themfelves. It has been faid that they litterally followed the principles of archbifhop *Laud*, which had caufed the troubles in the late reign, and this law evidently correfponds with that affertion. Whether many of them were at this time court penfioners feems to me fomewhat doubtful: but of the king it may be faid, that about the time of making this act he negotiated with *Lewis* XIV. in order to receive a fum of money " by way of loan, to affift him in his preffing neceffities, which " would not permit him, without very confiderable prejudice, to wait

" the

" the payment of the gratifications of his parliament," [z]—that he sold *Dunkirk* to *France* to supply his profusion—that in the early part of his reign he acquiesced in the injurious and dangerous seizure which the *French* king made of *Placentia* in *Newfoundland*—that in the year 1667, by the treaty of *Breda*, he ceded to *France Nova Scotia*, the ancient and rightful inheritance of his crown, whose chief value was derived from its relation to the fishery, and which *Cromwel* having by arms restored to the kingdom, *France* by her force or arts could never regain during his usurpation—that in the latter part of his reign he submitted to the notorious encroachment made on a considerable part of the sea-coast of the *American* continent belonging to the *English*, by the *French* king, who in support of this encroachment, and in open defiance of all right and justice, seized and confiscated the *English* fishing vessels at his pleasure; and having during his exile applied himself particulary to navigation, and the building of ships, in which he had made great progress, bishop *Burnet* writes thus, " His contributing so much to the raising the great-
" ness of *France*, chiefly at sea, was such an error; that it could not
" flow from want of thought, or of true sense. *Rouvigny* told me he
" desired that all the methods the *French* took in the increase and con-
" duct of their naval force might be sent him.   And, he said, he seemed
" to study them with concern and zeal.   He shewed what errors they
" committed, and how they ought to be corrected, as if he had been a
" viceroy to *France*, rather than a king that ought to have watched over
" and prevented the progress they made, as the greatest of all the mischiefs
" that could happen to him, or to his people [a]."   And in the reign of king *James* II. the *French* king avowed and maintained his encroachments on the *English* fishing ground on the continent, and continued his usurpations upon *Newfoundland*, and the fishery there, without molestation of king *James*, who with his ancestors neglecting to preserve and support the rights of the *English* in this important quarter, the *French* encouraged by their various acquisitions formed in this reign a design of making themselves entire masters of the *American* cod-fishery, which originally of right belonged to the *English*—How far these injurious

[z] *D'Estrades* Letters, Vol. 1st .   [a] History. of his own Time, Vol. i. p. 614.

proceedings

proceedings required thofe free expoftulations and reprefentations which the truftees of the people had fo feverely reftrained I fhall fubmit to the judicious and impartial reader, without confidering the defign or attempts of king *James* to fubvert the religion liberty and laws of his kingdom, which called for the nobleft efforts of the moft heroic minds to expofe them, and for the effectual profecution whereof fuch doctrines touching libels were advanced on the kings behalf, and fupported by feveral of his judges, as by their admiffion and operation would, I conceive, ferve to cenfure and condemn every writing relative to the ftate that fhould be difagreeable to any prince, however innocent or laudable they might be.

But addreffing myfelf again to the ecclefiaftic *Roman* emperours, whofe tyranny was ever accompanied and ftrengthened by their confident claim to divine infpiration and infallibility, and whofe cruelties were ever exercifed in the name of Almighty God, the fountain of all goodnefs, whofe laws are founded in righteoufnefs, juftice, equity and mercy, notwithftanding their empire was fupported by the moft refined policy and fuch numerous forces, with what was ftill more powerful, the violent prejudices of the people, at length Truth being introduced by Time, affifted by her intelligent and faithful friends, they, being in fome places permitted to appear and act with vigour, and in others through the noblenefs of her caufe, and the excellence of their fortitude, facing all dangers, and breaking through all reftraints, affailed thefe tyrants with fuch judgment force and fpirit, that they refcued feveral nations out of bondage, and reftored them to the dominion of truth, which makes all men as free as is confiftent with their welfare, and fhaking this tyranny to its foundations reduced the tyrants to that better conduct which from their plenary eftablifhment they never obferved but through neceffity; and I prefume that knowledge of the truth, to which a free enquiry is requifite, is as neceffary to the enjoyment of civil as religious rights. With refpect to the paffages cited from the Holy Scriptures, they will not fupport the ftar-chamber refolution for rejecting the truth, of which they make no mention; but, inftead of a tedious and unneceffary difcuffion of thefe feveral paffages, after obferving that the inhibition to curfe the ruler of the people contained in the law of *Mofes*, appears to
me

me to be of univerfal and perpetual obligation, the common good of every ftate requiring that, inftead of curfing, the fubjects fhould revere and honour their chief ruler as far as may be, whofe title to this defirable reverence and honour will at all times, I conceive, be beft fecured by his paternal conduct, I fhall in defence of truth adduce the following paffages. " Thou cameft down alfo upon mount *Sinai*, and fpakeft " with them from heaven; and gaveft them right judgments, and *true* " laws, good ftatutes and commandments." *Nehem :* ix : 13. " By " mercy and truth iniquity is purged." *Prov.* xvi: 6. " Wo unto them " that call evil good, and good evil; that put darknefs for light, and " light for darknefs ; that put bitter for fweet, and fweet for bitter :" *Ifaiah* v : 20. " they are not valiant for the truth upon the earth ; for " they proceed from evil to evil, and they know not me, faith the " Lord." *Jerem.* ix: 3. " We are fure that the judgment of God is " according to truth." *Rom.* ii: 2. For we can do nothing againft the " truth, but for the truth." 2 *Cor.* xiii : 8. All free and lawful governments are founded in truft, and frame your government as you pleafe, after completing your politic with the aid of the wifdom and experience of all ages and nations, for its execution it will finally reft in truft. *Donec homines erunt vitia*; and notwithftanding the facred nature of this truft the hiftories of all countries too clearly prove that authority is apt to run into power, and power into tyranny ; wherefore the ufe of every mean of preventing this malady is defirable : and one of the chief points of excellence of the *Britifh* conftitution confifting in the frequent opportunities which it gives to the people to chufe new truftees, a faithful reprefentation of the conduct of the former, and of the ftate of the times, which may loudly call for the choice of men of the greateft honour, fenfe and experience, with fuch diligence as to delight in examining to the bottom every point of public welfare, without confiding in the reprefentation of others, which may be imperfect, erroneous, or illufory, may excite their ferious confideration, with fuch choice as may fuit the occafion, and the noble privilege they enjoy.

From what has been faid, with the readers farther reflections, it will, I apprehend, plainly appear that in many cafes of great importance the liberty of the prefs may well be employed in promoting the interefts,

preventing

preventing the impending mifchiefs, or redreffing the grievances of pub-lic focieties, wherein no other means can be purfued to any effect, and in many other cafes an affiftant to proper meafures profecuted for the advance-ment of the public welfare; and it is needlefs to fay that thefe advanta-ges are to be derived from the illuftration and maintenance of truth againft all opponents; neverthelefs, with refpect to the ftar-chamber doctrine, that the truth of a writing profecuted as a libel is not mate-rial, I fhall farther obferve, 1, that the author of " The Doctrine of Libels difcuffed", who feems to have fearched into all *English* antiquity for precedents of judgments given in violent times, to be produced *in terrorem*; for he adduces feveral which, by his own confeffion, are not law at this day, among other things, writes thus in his introduction; " but undoubtedly flanders which might do mifchief, [words of great " latitude] whether true or falfe, were punifhable by the old common " law," without fhewing one precedent or authority for this purpofe; and lord *Coke*, or the ftar-chamber judges, having produced none to this effect, it may be concluded, I conceive, that there are none to be found. 2, that during the exiftence of the ftar-chamber court, as well as fince, it feems to have been a point fully fettled that in actions of flander the defendant might well juftify his fpeaking of the flanderous words charged upon him, by an averment that they were true. 3, that fpeech and writ-ing are not of contrary natures, but differ only in degree of certainty and permanence, and in the mode of conveying to the intellect the fame ob-ject of confideration; wherefore I confefs it has ever appeared ftrange to me that the fame truth fhould be lawful when orally delivered, and cri-minal when reduced into writing. 4. Lord *Coke*, in his 2d. Inftitute, calls truth the mother of juftice; and afterwards he cites, with approbation, this old and excellent rule, *veritas, à quocunque dicitur, a Deo eft*. " Truth, " by whomfoever fpoken, is from God." 5. that on the tryal of the feven bifhops for a libel, in prefenting their petition to the king, Mr. juftice *Powell*, who by his conduct acquired perpetual honour; after hearing this ftar-chamber cafe *de libellis famofis* cited and relied on, and every thing that was poffible faid for the rejection of truth, as immaterial, fpoke thus to the jury. " Gentlemen, to make it a libel it muft be falfe; " it muft be malicious; and it muft tend to fedition."

The

The ftar chamber refolution touching the indifference of truth was fuitable to their other conduct, being in effect a law made in their own defence. On the 17th. of October, when fitting at the council-table, they had concurred with the king in that fevere and indignant order which he publifhed refpecting the merchants importing tobacco; and in Eafter term following, when fitting in the court of ftar-chamber, they made this refolution, whereby they fubjected fuch fuffering merchants as fhould in writing complain of any part of their conduct relative to this illegal proceeding to fuch farther fines and punifhments as they fhould think fit to impofe.

The definition given of a libel in this ftar-chamber cafe, fo far as re-lates to the prefent purpofe, without confidering the point of falfity, feems rather imperfect, to wit, A fcandalous libel *in fcriptis* is when a writing is compofed or publifhed to the fcandal or contumely of another, which words do not neceffarily include the evil intent of the writer; but may relate to the cafual or undefigned effect of the writing. The defini-tion cited from *Bracton*, and by him taken from *Juftinians* Inftitutes, does not contain the words *dolove malo fecerit quo quid eorum fieret*, which made part of *Juftinians* definition. I mention this for the fake of the next point to be confidered, the malice of the writer, with its proof, whofe place many would fupply with prefumption. Dr. *Ridley* [b] fays " A fa-" mous libel is where a man hath of malitious purpofe writ, compoun-" ded, or fet out any thing to the infamie of another, without a name, " or with a name." Serj[t]. *Hawkins* fays, " That a libel in a ftrict fenfe " is taken for a malicious defamation, expreffed either in printing or " writing, and tending either to blacken the memory of one who is " dead, or the reputation of one who is alive, and to expofe him to public " hatred, contempt, or ridicule [c]."

With refpect to the malice of the writer, *Schulting*, in his *Juris pru-dentia Vetus, Ante-juftinianea*, upon the words of *Caius*[a], *aut injuriam fecerit*, explained by the comment of *Aleander*, " By hand, or words, " or writings," gives the following comment of *Oifelius*. " Now to do " an injury it is required that fome of thofe things which we have fpoken

[a] Caii. In-ftit.lib. ii. tit. 10.

[b] View of the Civil and Ecclef. Law, P. I. Ch. i. Sect. 9.   [c] Pleas of the Crown, B. I. Ch. lxxiii. Sect. 1.

" be

" be done for the fake of contumely, and with a defire of doing an injury;
" for if an intent to do an injury be wanting it pertaineth not to this
" action. Moreover it is alfo requifite that the perfon be innocent to
" whom the injury is done." Mr. juftice *Holloway*, in the cafe of the
feven bifhops, obferved to the jury that " the end and intention of every
" action is to be confidered," and then applied this rule to their cafe.
Sir *George Mackenzie* writes thus, " He who finds an infamous libel,
" and fhews it, tho' to one only, is punifhable, if malice or defign can
be proved, elfe not; for there is nothing more ordinary, nor more inno-
" cently done, for the moft part, than to fhew fuch libels. Whether
" *dolus malus & animus injuriandi* (a defign to offend) be prefumed in
" this delict, or muft be proved, is much controverted. *Bertaz. confil.*
" 237. affirms that it is prefumed. *Farin.* quæft. 295. affirms it is not
" prefumed, but muft be proved: and I encline to this laft opinion,
feeing infamous libels are not now fo much refented as formerly, cuftom
having much allayed the pique which ufed to enfue thereupon; and that
" cuftom defends from all guilt in this cafe is moft learnedly maintained
" by *Coler*, decis. 154. where it was found that ftationers were abfolved,
" though they fold infamous libels, becaufe all ftationers ufe to fell
" fuch [d]." In the cafe of Dr. *Brown*. Trin. 5. *Annæ* B. R. in an
information againft him for a libel called " The country parfons advice
" to my Lord Keeper," it was held that an information will lye for
fpeaking ironically; " and Mr. Attorney faid 'twas laid to be wrote
" *ironicè*, and he ought to have fhewed at the trial that he did not
" intend to fcandalize them; and the jury are judges *quo animo* this was
" done, and they have found the ill intent [e]."

With refpect to the trial by jury of the party accufed of writing a libel,
the jurors, I prefume, are competent judges of the falfity, malice, and
the fact of writing, of the book, pamphlet or paper in queftion, with its
contents. This, I apprehend, correfponds with their original inftitution.
Several learned perfons have fuppofed that trials by jury have taken place
in *England* from time immemorial, whereas it feems probable that they
were introduced in the time of *Ethelred;* who, according to the *Savillian*

[d] Vol. II. Tit. 30. §. 5.   [e] 11th. Modern. The Queen v. *Brown.*

account,

account, began his reign in the year 979, and died in the year 1016, to whofe reign the following ordinance is referred. *In fingulis centuriis comitia funto, atque liberæ conditionis viri duodeni, ætate fuperiores, una cum præpofito facra tenentes jurento, fe adeo virum aliquem innocentem haud damnaturos, fontemve abfoluturos.* Lord *Coke* cites this ancient record from *Lambard,* faving the words, *fe adeo virum aliquem innocentem haud damnaturos, fontemve abfoluturos.* Monsʳ *Argot* fays that about this time the inhabitants of towns and cities in *France* obtained the privilege of being tried by their peers; this cuftom being probably begun by the inhabitants of epifcopal cities and other free-men. Every crime is the tranfgreffion of fome law, the judgment whereof neceffarily comprizes the law, with the fact; and as all perfons are prefumed to know the laws, and are therefore punifhable for the breach of them, fo the jurors when a breach fhould come in queftion were prefumed to have knowledge fuitable to their inftitution. By the great charter it is provided that no free-man fhall be condemned but by lawful judgment of his peers, whereby, in the plaineft terms, effectual provifion is made that every man when charged with a crime fhall be tried by his peers, who have power to condemn or abfolve him, this provifion being apparently made as well for the commons as the peers of the realm.

The defire of king *James* to introduce and eftablifh the papal tyranny with his own was fo vehement, that he could not brook the noble check which the feven bifhops gave to the progrefs of his fuperftition and ambition; whereupon the profecution againft them as libellers for having petitioned his majefty in the moft decent and proper manner to excufe their non compliance with his illegal command took place; for the maintenance whereof every argument that could be devifed was urged. *Wright,* chief juftice, whom Dr. *Burnet* calls the proper tool of the court, after fpeaking to the facts relative to the making and publifhing their petition, proceeding to enquire whether this petition was a libel, or not, declared to the jury that in his opinion it was a libel, adding that this being a point of law, if his brothers had any thing to fay to it, he fuppofed they would deliver their opinions; and Mr. juftice *Allybone* began his fpeech thus. " The fingle queftion that falls to my fhare is to give my fenfe " of this petition, whether it fhall be in conftruction of law a libel in " itfelf,

" itfelf, or a thing of great innocence ;" and after advancing thefe prepo-
fitions, 1, " that no man can take upon himfelf to write againft the
" actual exercife of the government, unlefs he has leave from the go-
" vernment, but he makes a libel, be what he writes true or falfe.
" 2. That no private man can take upon him to write concerning the
" government at all;" and giving his reafons, fuitable to his pofitions,
he clearly held this petition to be a libel; neverthelefs not one judge upon
the bench queftioned the propriety of the juries judging of the whole
matter, and giving a general verdict thereupon, though it has of late
been publickly infifted that they ought to have found a fpecial verdict,
and not taken upon them to determine whether this petition was a
libel or not.

In *Bufhells* cafe, 22 *Car.* II. [*f*], the nature of the trial by jury was
thoroughly examined and confidered by the court of common pleas,
and upon conference with all the judges. Upon a writ of *habeas corpus*
iffued by that court, on behalf of *Edward Bufhell*, and directed to the
fheriffs of *London*, they returned that at the court of oyer and terminer,
held for the city of *London* at juftice hall in the *Old Baily*, he was committed to the goal of *Newgate*, by virtue of an order of that court,
whereby it was ordered that a fine of 40 marks fhould be feverally impofed on him and eleven other perfons, being the twelve jurors fworn and
charged to try feveral iffues joined between the king and *William Penn*
and *William Mead*, for certain trefpaffes, contempts, unlawful affemblies
and tumults made and perpetrated by them, together with divers other
unknown perfons, to the number of three hundred, unlawfully and tu-
multuoufly affembled in *Grace-Church-ftreet*, to the difturbance of the
peace, whereof the faid *Penn* and *Mead* were then indicted, to which
indictment they pleaded not guilty; for that they the faid jurors the faid
Penn and *Mead* of the faid trefpaffes &c. contrary to the law of the kingdom, to full and manifeft evidence, and to the direction of the court in
the matter of law, in court openly given and declared, acquited, in contempt of the king and his laws, and to the great obftruction of juftice,
as alfo to the evil example of all other jurors offending in the like cafe;

[*f*] *Vaughans* Reports.

and

and becaufe the faid *Edward* had not paid the fine aforefaid he had til that time been detained in the faid goal. " Upon this return all the " judges refolved, That finding againſt the evidence in court, or direction " of the court barely, was no fufficient caufe to fine ;" and the fine, comitment, and imprifonment in this cafe being declared illegal, the prifoners were difcharged.

According to the courfe of the law, from the earlieſt times juries, I conceive, have had it in their power, upon the general iffue pleaded, to give a general verdict in civil as well as criminal caufes, although matter of law were complicated with the fact. By the ſtat. of Weſtmʳ. II. ᵃ it was " ordained that the juſtices affigned to take affizes ſhall not ᵃ13 Edw.I. " compel the jurors to fay precifely whether it be diffeifin, or not, fo " that they do ſhew the truth of the deed, and require aid of the juſtices. " But if they of their own head will fay that it is diffeifin, their verdict " ſhall be admitted at their own peril," *Littleton* ᵇ fays. " Alfo in fuch ᵇ§. 368. " cafe where the enqueſt may give their verdict at large, if they will take " upon them the knowledge of the law upon the matter, they may give " their verdict generally, as is put in their charge ;" whereon lord *Coke* comments thus. " Although the jury, if they will take upon them (as " *Littleton* here faith) the knowledge of the law, may give a general " verdict, yet it is dangerous for them fo to do ; for if they do miſtake " the law they run into the danger of an attaint ; therefore to find the " fpecial matter is the fafeſt way, where the cafe is doubtful."

Lord chief juſtice *Vaughan*, to whom, with the other judges, in my poor opinion, the kingdom will ever be obliged, for eſtabliſhing the right of juries to give general verdicts in criminal caufes, as well as to the prefent lord chief juſtice of the fame court, and the other judges, who have declared general warrants to be illegal, in *Buſhells* cafe, obferves that, " Upon all general iffues ; as upon not culpable pleaded in trefpafs, " *nil debet* in debt, *nul tort, nul diffeifin* in affize, *ne diſturba pas* in *Quare* " *impedit,* and the like ; though it be matter of law whether the defend- " ant be a trefpaffor, a debtor, diffeifor, or diſturber in the particular " cafes in iffue ; yet the jury find not (as in a fpecial verdict) the fact " of every cafe by itfelf, leaving the law to the court, but find for the " plaintiff or defendant upon the iffue to be tryed, wherein they re- " folve

" folve both law and fact complicately, and not the fact by itfelf;
" fo as though they anfwer not fingly to the queftion what is law, yet
" they determine the law in all matters where iffue is joined, and tryed in
" the principal cafe, but where the verdict is fpecial."

We have in part feen to what great dangers and mifchiefs the fubjects
are expofed when trials by their peers are fubverted, and other modes of
trial introduced; wherefore it is extremely defirable that trials by jury
fhould ever be equal, fair and free, influenced by truth of fact and argument only; fo that, with the affiftance of thofe excellent judges to whofe
opinions proper regard fhould be had, they may be as perfect as the
nature of human affairs will permit; and to this end, among other wife
provifions, to free them from all apprehenfions of danger attendant on
the difcharge of their duty, according to ferj*. *Hawkins,* [g] " it feemeth
" to be certain, That no one is liable to any profecution whatfoever, in
" refpect of any verdict given by him in a criminal matter, either upon
" a grand or petit jury; for fince the fafety of the innocent, and punifh-
" ment of the guilty, doth fo much depend upon the fair and upright
" proceeding of jurors, it is of the utmoft confequence that they fhould
" be as little as poffible under the influence of any paffion whatfoever.
" And therefore, left they fhould be biaffed with the fear of being har-
" raffed by a vexatious fuit, for acting according to their confciences (the
" danger of which might eafily be infinuated where powerful men are
" warmly engaged in a caufe, and thoroughly prepoffeffed of the juftice
" of the fide which they efpoufe) the law will not leave any poffibility
" for a profecution of this kind. It is true indeed the jurors were for-
" merly fometimes queftioned in the ftar-chamber, for their partiality
" in finding a manifeft offender not guilty; but this was always thought
" a very great grievance; and furely as the law is now fettled by *Bufhells*
" cafe, there is no kind of proceeding againft jurors in refpect of their
" verdicts in criminal matters allowed of at this day."

The mifchiefs of flander confift in its operation on the minds of perfons, with their confequent actions; and it feems to me that jurors are
well qualified to judge of the whole, efpecially when affifted by able and

[g] Pleas of the Crown, B. I. Ch. lxxvi. §. 5.

                                                    " impartial

impartial judges. In cafe a perpetual fucceffion of judges equal to thofe excellent perfons who now fit in the feat of judgment could be fecured to the kingdom we might be lefs follicitous touching this particular : but although through his majeftys goodnefs provifion has been made that his own fon, or any future fucceffor, fhall not have it in his power on his acceffion to appoint new judges at his pleafure ; yet it is poffible that future times may produce fuch men as being devoted to the will of arbitrary princes, or dangerous minifters, fhall be ready to ufe every mean in their power to reftrain and punifh thofe writings which may be neceffary to expofe their defigns ; and it being difficult in thefe times of danger to ftem the current of thofe precedents whereof an ill ufe may be made, the practice of giving general verdicts, I conceive, may contribute to the prefervation of the liberty of the prefs, which hath in times paft been fo feverely reftrained by law, or lawlefs power. *Julius Cæfar* obferved that the moft dangerous precedents are made in favorable cafes, and we have lately feen even office precedents urged with vehemence to warrant the violation of the law of liberty and fafety, by men who have fince unhappily proved that their caution was not encreafed by the correction of their errors.

Notwithftanding the great utility of the liberty of the prefs it is certainly liable to manifold injurious abufes, fometimes pregnant with great mifchiefs ; without enumerating others, inftead of being helpful to preferve, it may be employed by our enemies to divide and deftroy us ; wherefore juft and proper bounds are to be obferved. Every confiderate and fincere friend to the freedom of writing laments thefe abufes perpetrated by the various enemies of the public weal. *Libertas non eft licentia* fays *Tacitus*, the great friend of liberty, railing is not reafoning, nor are invectives arguments ; vague and general reproaches, charges and criminations may injure, provoke, and inflame, but they neither rightly inform, nor reform. The caufe of truth and juftice is not promoted by obloquy and detraction, the *decus & tutamen* of the common-wealth is not to be affailed by petulance and impertinence ; yet, inftead of proper examination and reprefentation, fuch a licentious ufe of the prefs hath taken place, that neither the higheft public ftations, nor the greateft public fervices, nor public nor private virtues, nor the abfence of the

fufferers,

sufferers, are sufficient guards against these abuses. All personal, provincial and national abuse is the prostitution of the press, and may sometimes produce great and mischievous effects. *Juncta juvant*, and in
interesting cases the errors of politicians, with the errors and incentives
of pamphleteers, encreased and diffused by that *cacoethes scribendi & male
dicendi* which delights in defaming, aggravating and inflaming, instead
of duly considering, informing, and composing, and, as the seeds of
social as well as natural diseases generate apace, spreading far and wide
a political pestilence, prejudice begeting prejudice, and error begeting
error, and the whole producing violence, opposition, division and confusion, may, without the co-operation of the dangerous devices suggested
by others to effectuate their deep and malignant designs, subject the most
powerful state to great difficulties. Of this we have at present an instance
so alarming in its nature, and uncertain in its consequences that it calls,
in my poor opinion, for the closest examination, and the most calm just
and equal consideration, so that being understood in its origin, progress,
and present state, all future evils may as far as possible be prevented, for
the accomplishment whereof every good subject, I presume, will chear-
fully contribute what lies in his power. I need not explain myself by
naming the colonies, whose nature, rights, and interests, considered in
themselves, and in their connection with their mother country, have
been so egregiously misrepresented by numerous public writers in this
metropolis, and in the colonies, many of whom have advanced proposi-
tions utterly incompatible with the nature of the *British* empire, and
subversive of it, some oppugning the supreme authority of the state, and
others the just rights of *British* subjects. And having perhaps taken
more pains than any of my fellow citizens to understand the nature and
rights of colonies, ancient and modern, and of the *English* colonies in
particular, so that my defects in point of natural abilities are in some
measure supplied by my diligence, I shall in order to illustrate this important subject, with the best intensions for the public service, submit some
few things to public consideration, with all due deference to my supe-
riours in every sense, proceeding, as far as may be with convenience, by
way of proposition, in order that the truth may be more clearly comprehended, and readily embraced, and my involuntary errors more easily
refuted,

refuted, whereby I fhall hope to avoid encreafing the number of thofe who enter and traverfe the field of controverfy without the direction of any certain principle. All arguments deftitute of proper principles are mere empty fophifms; they may captivate and delude, but they can neither duly inform nor promote the public welfare; and yet we daily fee writers on both fides of the *Atlantic* proceeding with an air of fufficiency to treat of the political ftructure of the colonies, or fome of its parts, without either knowing or enquiring into its real proper and folid foundation, the right underftanding whereof might prevent innumerable mifchiefs. Truth is fimple and uniform, and ever attended with a happy coincidence of all its parts, whereas error is infinite. And, in order to afcertain the beft mode of inveftigating the truth, thereby cuting off many delufive arguments, I fhall cite the excellent rule delivered and maintained by the learned and judicious *Placcius,* viz. *Demonftraturum quid de re aliqua, eandem in perfectiffimo gradu confiderare debere.* " That " he who would demonftrate any thing relative to any fubject, ought to confider that in the moft perfect degree."

AMERICA, fince difcovered by the *Europeans,* hath fuffered greatly by various political errors; through prejudice, with its confequents injuftice and cruelty, *Spain* flew her millions, of whom fhe might, to the great encreafe of her honour, wealth and ftrength, have made good fubjects, or profitable allies. Continuing under the dominion of prejudice, and transfering her pernicious policy to *Europe,* by her injuftice and feverity fhe loft the *Netherlands,* and by her manifold breaches of faith, and oppreffions, fhe loft the kingdom of *Portugal,* with all its foreign dominions, every colony, fort and fettlement (adhering firmly, as was natural, to their mother country) revolting with her, *Ceuta,* and fome of the iflands of the *Azores,* garrifoned by *Spanifh* foldiers, only excepted. *Spain,* if influenced by the fole dictates of juftice and equity, would have preferved the *Americans,* and held the *Netherlands,* with all the dominions of *Portugal,* firmly united to her by the ftrongeft bonds, faith and love, whereby, with fuitable policy, fhe might have raifed the moft glorious empire, exceeding all modern example, and common conception. Rational liberty, and equal juftice, plenty and fafety, being the chief ends of all lawful government, the mifconduct of *Spain,* with its confequences,

quences, will, to all ages and nations, irrefiftably prove againft a thoufand authors who join hand in hand to countenance dark devices, and
promote iniquity, that the principle of univerfal felicitation is the beft
mean of prefervation and aggrandizement.   And now, without vifiting
the *American* dominions of other *European* princes, coming *per faltum* to
Britifh America, whofe prefent and future ftate fo nearly concerns the
common-weal, it prefents a moft unpleafing fcene.   It was lately the
feat of a fharp and cruel war, waged by thofe enemies who never give
us farther reft than their inability inforces, with intent to wreft from us
one of the chief fources of our commercial and naval empire, during the
courfe whereof feveral colonies raifed a larger proportion of men than
any other part of his majefty's dominions; and fince, while labouring to
reftore the broken ftate of their affairs, and to profecute that trade which
is fo neceffary to the commerce of this kindom, through the fudden
change of *Britifh* policy, and a ftrange feries of errors and events, the
whole are now plunged into a ftate of diftrefs, difficulty and danger, from
which it is defirable in fo many refpects to deliver them as foon as poffible,
and to fhew their true political foundation, in order to their complete and
perpetual union with this kingdom, for the common good.   The eftablifhment, corroboration and prefervation of this union, confidered in its
moft perfect degree, will appear, I prefume, to every impartial and confiderate perfon worthy of the greateft attention.   The diftant fituation of
the colonies, with their cantonment and diftinct civil adminiftrations,
though placed under the wife and provident care which prefides over all
parts of the ftate, raifes infenfibly in the minds of many worthy perfons
partial notions difcordant with this union; but its greateft enemy, I conceive, is prejudice, that malady of the mind, and powerful director of
its motions; and in this cafe, as well as in that of fuperftition, unfortunately wife men frequently follow fools, and our infular and conti-
nental prejudices are become fo numerous and violent, that I who am fo
feeble an advocate for the principles of truth, univerfal juftice, and public
welfare, the fole proper and firm foundation, in my poor opinion, of that
lafting and profitable union that is fo much to be defired by all good
citizens, dare not enter the lift againft fo formidable an enemy; and
therefore adhering to my principle of peace, and that uniting, conciliating

                                                                        and

and ftrengthening fyftem which I have ever held, after obferving that common juftice is the common debt due to and from all perfons and focieties, and the common caufe of all honeft men, and that nothing can be more unreafonable than for a man to make one law in his mind for himfelf, and another for other perfons, I fhall defire the favour of him who on reading what has been faid refpecting this perfect union fhall perceive the leaft prejudice to arife in his mind againft it, that he will be pleafed calmly to confider this divine precept of the Saviour of the world, " all things whatfoever ye would that men fhould do to you, " do ye even fo to them, for this is the law and the prophets," And if this fhall not fuffice to efface the impreffions of prejudice, that he will lay afide this little effay until he come to fuch a temper of mind that he fhall be willing to do as he would be done unto; in the mean time, accompanied by the favour of the candid reader, I fhall proceed to obferve,

Mat. vii. 12.

I. That his majeftys regal authority extends to all perfons, and over all parts of the public territory—that every fubject by the law and the duties of his birth is obliged to be faithful, and bear true allegiance to the king—That allegiance and protection being correlatives, every fubject is entitled to protection.

II. That the nature of human government, in order to its comple-tion, of neceffity requires in every ftate for its welfare and prefervation the exiftence and occafional exercife of a fupreme legiflative jurifdiction, over all and fingular the parts, perfons natural corporate or compound, caufes, matters and things whatfoever—That by the *Britifh* conftitution this fupreme jurifdiction is vefted in the *Britifh* parliament—That the entire collective dominion, ftate, or chief body politic, compofed of all its members, admits but of one fupreme direction, equals have no power over equals, and two or more fupreme jurifdictions cannot be erected without forming two or more different ftates; and it is evident this divi-fion minifters to deftruction. The colonies from their fituation, nature, and neceffary political exiftence poffefs fubordinate powers of legiflation, but the fole *fummum imperium* of the *Britifh* parliament remains firm, immutable and univerfal—That the kings juft prerogative was ever parcel of the law of the land; and, to ufe the words of lord *Bacon*, who,

with

with other able lawyers and ftates men, was much confulted and concerned in the fettlement of fome of the colonies. " The kings preroga-
" tive and the law are not two things"—" There is not in the body of
" man one law of the head and another of the body; but all is one
" entire law." And it is certain that none of his majeftys predeceffors
had it in their power by any act made *de induftria* in any manner whatever to diminifh the jurifdiction of parliament, or to divide that body
politic of which they were the head, thereby making a change nearly
affecting the royal prerogative together with the whole common-wealth.
Nil dat quod non habet is a maxim of law, philofophy and common fenfe,
and no colonic or other politic body can by force of any charter claim
any power, privilege or jurifdiction exempt from parliamentary cognizance, the king having no authority to raife or create the fame. Every
charter is the creature of the law, and neceffarily fubject to the law and
the law-makers; and we have too much reafon to remember the ancient
and juft obfervation, *Ordo confunditur fi unicuique jurifdictio non fer-
vetur.*

III. That the nature and intent of parliamentary jurifdiction, I prefume, are to declare and enact what is right, equal and juft, giving to
the common-wealth and its various parts their due. Ancient authors
declare verity and juftice to be the proper foundation of parliamentary
proceedings. *Jurifdictio eft poteftas de publico, introducta cum neceffitate
juris dicendi* [*b*]; and lord *Coke* fays *jurifdictio* is derived of *jus & ditio*, i.
poteftas juris. And although through prejudice, paffion or other infirmities
men may not in particular cafes, efpecially when their minds are moved
by felf-intereft, difcern and diftinguifh between truth and error, juftice
and injuftice; yet truth, juftice and equity are in their nature immutable,
and no more fubject to annihilation, inverfion, or variation, than any
geometrical propofition—That no prince, potentate, ftate or order of
men can by any means whatever acquire a right of doing what is wrong.
An author whofe exquifite learning, knowledge and judgment have done
fo great honour to human nature, as well as to this kingdom, Dr. *Cudworth,* hath clearly fhewn that even in pofitive laws and commands it is

[*b*] See the proem to *Cokes* 4th Inftit.

not

not meer will that obligeth, but the nature of good and evil, juft and unjuft, really exifting. In the courfe of his reafoning he writes thus, " every thing is what it is by nature, and not by will; for though it " will be objected here that when God or civil powers command a " thing to be done that was not before *obligatory or unlawful,* the thing " willed or commanded doth forthwith become *obligatory,* that which " ought to be done by creatures and fubjects refpectively; in which the " nature of moral good or evil is commonly conceived to confift ; and " therefore if all good and evil, juft and unjuft be not the creatures of " meer will (as many affert) yet at leaft *pofitive things* muft needs owe " all their morality, their good and evil to meer will without nature ; " yet notwithftanding, if we well confider it, we fhall find that even " in pofitive commands themfelves meer will doth not make the thing " commanded juft or obligatory, or beget and create any obligation to " obedience ; but that it is natural juftice or equity which gives to one " the right or authority of commanding, and begets in another duty and obligation to obedience [*i*]."—According to Dr. *Cumberlands* excellent rule, approved, or rather applauded by the moft eminent foreign authors, " Nothing can be deemed the law of nature in which all men cannot " agree"; and the moft able jurifts have united in declaring that pofitive focial laws fhould inforce the natural, or conform to them as far as poffible. Mr. *Locke* fays, " The obligations of the law of nature ceafe " not in fociety, but only in many cafes are drawn clofer, and have by " human laws known penalties annexed to them to inforce their obfer- " vation. Thus the law of nature ftands as an eternal rule to all men, " *legiflators* as well as others, The rules that they make for other mens " actions muft, as well as their own and other mens actions, be con- " formable to the law of nature, *i. e.* to the will of God, of which " that is a declaration." And that " the firft and fundamental pofitive " law of all common-wealths is the eftablifhing the legiflative power, " as the firft and fundamental natural law, which is to govern even the " legiflative itfelf, is the prefervation of the fociety, and (as far as will

[*i*] Treatife concerning internal and imutable Morality, p. 17, 18.

" confift

" confift with the public good) of every perfon in it [*k*]."—That good and perfect laws are the dictates of perfect reafon relative to their fub- ject known in all its parts; and pofitive laws, fo far as they partake of prejudice, paffion, improvidence, or other infirmity, or are formed on the partial knowledge of their refpective fubjects, are imperfect; the wifeft legiflators cannot judge aright, or rather not at all, of that which was never expofed to their judgment, and a law made upon the beft confidera- tion of fome parts only of its fubject matter, with an exclufion or infcience of other proper and material or effential parts, from the nature of legi- flation, and its objects, is apparently an improper or imperfect law. Confidered with refpect to the cafe ftated and fuppofed, if the fame had fubfifted, it might have been juft and proper; but the true and real cafe, compofed of all its parts, materially differing from it, required either a different law, or none at all; and confequently the law thus made through error, according to the immutable principles of truth, juftice, and legiflation, I prefume, is to be difcontinued, the continuance of an error when known differing widely from its firft commiffion when un- known; neverthelefs it is the duty of the parties concerned to obey fuch erroneous or improper law as far as poffible, until its review and repeal by the legiflators fhall take place, to whofe wife, equal and juft confideration and decifion all reafons refpecting its real or fuppofed errors, improprieties or defects, muft be properly and entirely fubmitted.——— That the ableft politicians have held it difficult for one country to make laws for another; and the greater their diftance the greater their diffi- culty. The *Roman* councils were frequently embarraffed by this bufinefs, although their political wifdom fo far exceeded in many refpects that of other nations. The nature of the *Britifh* empire, divided by the fituation of its feveral parts, with the neceffary unity of the fupreme power over the whole, is inevitably accompanied with this difficulty. All the free- holders in *England* worthy of notice in this behalf are reprefented in par- liament by perfons chofen by them for that purpofe, who, with the re- prefentatives of the cities and boroughs, and the reprefentatives of

[*k*] Treatife of Government, Chap. 11th.

Scotland,

Scotland, form the houfe of commons, or an order of men well acquainted with the nature, condition and intereft of the whole kingdom, and its refpective parts ; and yet when interefting laws are depending how oft do we fee fpecial communications take place between thefe reprefentatives and their conftituents, for the fake of better information ; and notwithftanding the ufe of thefe, the beft means of knowledge, an improper or imperfect law has been fome times made : and when the principal or dominant part of a ftate makes a law relative to its diftant parts it feems defirable to ufe every mean of inveftigating the truth refpecting all the fubject matters of it, fo that the numerous additional difficulties unavoidably arifing from diftance may, as far as poffible, be countervailed by the moft diligent comprehenfive enquiry and thorough examination, without which provident care laws made for the advancement of commerce may caufe its diminution, and other laws may operate contrary to the intent of the legiflators ; and it is needlefs to fay that when fuch dominant part makes a law for the diftant parts in eafe of itfelf the moft liberal juft and equitable confideration becomes more efpecially requifite, in order to countervail the natural dictates of felf intereft. With refpect to the political ftate of our colonies there feems to be no bounds to the errors of minor politicians and pamphleteers, which, with other errors relating to their commercial ftate, joining and increafing the prejudices and tempeftuous paffions of numbers have caufed fo great violence and grievous outrages. In truth many of *Britannias* fons feem to have loft the proper fenfe of their duty to their mother and to each other, brother would baftardize brother, fome would unnaturalize others, and others would unnaturalize themfelves, without duly confidering their own conduct in its nature and confequences. To check thefe mifchiefs, and reftore all things into order, the chief ftrength and fafety, as well as beauty, of the civil ftate, I know no means fo ufeful as having recourfe to truth, the common friend of all honeft men, and of all juft meafures; and therefore returning to my former courfe of proceeding I fhall farther obferve,

IV. That the *Englifh* colonies are the legitimate off-fpring, image and part of the common-wealth, and well entitled to the rights, liberties, and benefits of it, or, in other words, they have good title to *jus publi-*

cum

cum and *jus privatum*, and to both *optimo jure*, the enlargement of the empire, in purfuance of proper regal authority, at the toil and peril, and the expenfe of the blood and treafure of the planters—That thefe rights entitle them of courfe to every proper and practicable mean of preferving them, rights without the means of their prefervation being defeafible and illufory—That by the firft leading grant made for the difcovery and fettlement of the *Englifh* part of *America* to Sir *Humphrey Gilbert* by queen *Elizabeth*, on the 21ft. day of June, in the 20th. year of her reign, after directing that the fame fhould be made by her *Englifh* and *Irifh* fubjects; for uniting in more perfect league and amity fuch countries " with her realms of *England* and *Ireland* and for the better encouraga-
" ment of men to this enterprize;" fhe granted and declared that all fuch countries fo to be poffeffed and inhabited fhould thenceforth be of the allegiance of her, her heirs and fucceffors, and did thereby grant to Sir *Humphrey*, his heirs and affigns, and to all other perfons of her allegiance, who fhould, in purfuance of the directions therein contained, proceed and inhabit within any fuch countries, that they and their heirs " fhould have and enjoy all the privileges of free denizens and perfons " native of *England*, and within her allegiance, in fuch like ample manner " and form as if they were born and perfonally refiaunte within the " faid realm of *England*."—That the grant made to Sir *Walter Ralegh*, under which the firft fettlement was made in *Virginia*, was in thefe refpects fimilar to this; and it is altogether unneceffary, I apprehend, to cite the feveral fucceeding royal grants which were grafted upon thefe, and co-operated with them in eftablifhing the *Englifh* empire in *America*, every fubfequent grant being made by the king of *England* to his fubjects, whether to an individual or to numbers, to perfons natural or politic, as well thofe which have loft their force as thofe which continue in force, in their nature and tenor fuppofing, confirming, and eftablifhing this empire, and ftrenthening the connection of thefe diftant countries, and all their inhabitants, with the realm of *England*, the king holding the whole under the fame allegiance—That by the ftat. 15 *Car.* II. cap. vii. which provided that the *European* commodities imported into the plantations fhould be fhiped in *England*, whofe policy and provifion I have heretofore laboured to preferve, it is thus recited and declared, " in regard
" his

" his majefties plantations beyond the feas are inhabited and peopled by his
" fubjects of this his kingdom of *England* : for the maintaining a greater
" correfpondence and kindnefs between them, and keeping them in a
" firmer dependence upon it, and rendring them yet more beneficial and
" advantageous unto it, in the further employment and increafe of
" *Englifh* fhiping and feamen, vent of *Englifh* woollen and other manu-
" factures and commodities, rendring the navigation to and from the
" fame more fafe and cheap, and making this kingdom a ftaple not
" only of the commodities of thofe plantations, but alfo of the commodi-
" ties of other countries and places, for the fupplying of them ; and it
" being the ufage of other nations to keep their plantation trade to
" themfelves : Be it enacted" &c. Here we have an exprefs declaration
made by parliament, *per verba de præfenti* ; that his majeftys plantations
beyond the feas were inhabited and peopled by his fubjects of this his
kingdom of *England*, whofe political ftate hath queftionlefs ever fince
continued the fame—That by the ftat. 13 *Geo.* II. cap. vii. it was enacted
that from and after the 1ft. day of June, in the year 1740, all perfons
born out of the ligeance of the king, his heirs and fucceffors, who had
inhabited, or fhould inhabit, for the fpace of feven years, or more in any
of his majeftys colonies in *America*, and fhould take the oaths, and make
the declarations therein directed, " fhould be deemed, adjudged, and
" taken to be his majefty's natural born fubjects of this kingdom, to all
" intents, conftructions and purpofes, as if they and every of them had
" been or were born within this kingdom."—That it is impoffible, I
conceive, for any prince or ftate intending to enlarge their public territory
by the acquifition of any diftant lands or countries, to take more proper
and efficacious means for making the fame parcel of their empire than
have from the foundation of the colonies been taken by the kings and
parliaments of *England* to unite them with their mother country, and
form one empire of the whole ; fo that confidering their nature, notoriety
and importance, it is matter of great furprize as well as concern, to fee
fuch manifold pertinacious miftakes made in this kingdom and the colonies
touching their political nature by numberlefs writers and other perfons,
who being ftrangers to their true foundation, form erroneous and injurious hypothefes concerning them.

With

V. With refpect to the queſtion when in a ſtate wherein the laws are made by the prince, the nobles, and perſons choſen by the people, the greater part live in one quarter of the world, and the leſſer part in another ; and the greater part chuſe thoſe perſons who make part of the legiſlative, and who are by the *Engliſh* lawyers and other authors, called the repreſentatives, attornies or advocates of their conſtituents, and in foreign ſtates ambaſſadours, or by other names denoting the perſons elected and deputed by many others, to repreſent and act for them, the leſſer part having no vote or voice in this choice, whether the perſons thus choſen by the greater part can be truly, juſtly and properly ſaid to be the repreſentatives of the leſſer part ; in which caſe I deſire leave to hold the negative, and pray the favour of him who is enclined to the affirmative, that he will conſider himſelf as one of the leſſer part, and then declare his approbation or diſapprobation of this repreſentation ; for in truth it ſeems to me that impartial conſideration might ſuffice to reſolve this queſtion ; nevertheleſs I ſhall endeavour to illucidate this particular.   It is ſaid that the *Engliſh* colonies, which are the leſſer part of the ſtate, though not actually, are virtually repreſented in par-liament by the members choſen by the greater part.   The miſchiefs, diviſions, difficulties and dangers which attend the ſtate, whoſe pri-mary ſource apparently was the conduct of miniſters unprovided with proper and neceſſary knowledge, with an excluſion of wiſer counſels, and better information, have ſeveral times brought to my mind *Pandoras* box, out of which the maladies and calamities of mankind took their flight. And truth being an immutable entity and intelligibility, and error a meer phantaſy or figment of the imagination, this notion of virtual re-preſentation being as incomprehenſible by my mental faculties as tran-ſubſtantiation, or the popes repreſentation of the Deity, hath brought to my mind the opinion of thoſe among the ancients who held that there was no certainty in the human intellect, or its objects : but on due con-ſideration, I am fully convinced, to uſe the words of Dr. *Cudworth*, that " Truth is the moſt unbending and uncompliable, the moſt neceſſary, " firm, immutable, and adamantine thing in the world ;" and in caſe this notion of virtual repreſentation be true, it is capable of being ſo clearly and diſtinctly repreſented and evinced as to force the aſſent of the equal

and

and intelligent mind; wherefore I hope that its advocates will be pleafed to explain, fupport and complete their new fyftem of reprefentation, obferving that equal rights require equal means of prefervation. That the inequalities in the reprefentation of one country are no reafon for rejecting the reprefentation of another. That according to the excellent rule of *Placcius*, and the fentiments of Mr. *Locke* in this particular, we are not to reafon from defect to defect, thereby making the political fyftem ftil more and more defective; but to keep the right line or ftate of perfection in view, making our approaches towards it, and that one plain fimple principle of univerfal juftice and public welfare is in my poor opinion, worth a thoufand fuch refinements or temporary expedients — That Mr. juftice *Doddridge*, that learned antiquary and able lawyer, fuppofes that the opinions of *Polydore Virgil* and *Paladine* are reconcileable with the "manufcript of *Canterbury*, that the firft parliament wherein the com- "mons were called, as well as the peers and nobles, was 16 *H. I.*; for it "is true that after the conqueft until this time the commons were not "called; and fo at this time they will have it firft called by the name of "a parliament." This learned judge calls *Edward* I. the founder of our civil ftate, and lord chief juftice *Hale* fays that he " is well ftiled our "*Englifh Juftinian*; for in his time the law *quafi per faltum* obtained a "very great perfection." And the following record will manifeft his fenfe of reprefentation.

Claus de Anno Regni regis Edwardi Viceffimo tertio.

Parliamento tenendo. "Rex venerabili in Chrifto patri "R. eadem gratia Cantuar archi- "pifcopo totius Angliæ primati Sa- "lutem. Sicut lex juftiffima pro- "vida circumfpectione facrarum "principium ftabilita hortatur, & "ftatuit, UT QUOD OMNES TAN- "GIT AB OMNIBUS APPROBETUR "fic et innuit evidenter ut com- "munibus periculis per remedia

The king to the venerable father in Chrift R. by the fame grace archbifhop of *Cant.* primate of all *England*, greeting. As the moft juft law by provident circumfpection of facred princes eftablifhed advifeth and hath appointed, THAT WHAT TOUCHETH ALL MEN BE APPROVED OF ALL, fo it likewife evidently intimateth that common "provifa

" provifa communiter obvietur fane
" fatis noftris et jam eft ut credi-
" mus p' univerfa mundi climata
" divulgatum qualiter rex Francie
" de terra noftra Vafconie nos cau-
" telofe decepit eum nobis nequi-
" ter detinendo nunc vero predictis
" fraude & nequicia non contentus
" ad expugnationem regni noftri
" claffe maxima & bellatorum co-
" piofa multitudine congregatis cum
" quibus regnum noftrum & regni
" ejufdem incolas hoftiliter jam in-
" vafit linguam Anglicam fi con-
" cepte iniquitatis propofito de
" teftabili poteftas correfpondeat
" quod Deus avertat omnino de
" terra delere proponat Quia igitur
" previfa jacula minus ledunt et res
" veftra maxima ficut ceterorum
" regni ejufdem concinium agitur
" in hac parte vobis mandamus in
" fide & dilectioni quibus nobis
" tenemini firmiter injungentes
" quod die dominica proxime poft
" feftum Sancti Martini in hyeme
" proxim' futur' apud Weftmo-
" nafterum perfonalit' interfitis pre-
" munientes priorem & capitulum
" ecclefie veftre archidiaconos to-
" tumque clerum veftre diocefis
" Facientes quod iidem prior & ar-
" chidiaconi in propriis perfonis
" fuis & dictum capitulum per
" unum idemque cleros per duos

danger be obviated by remedies provided with common confent. Truly we have as we think already fufficiently divulged through all climates of the world how the king of *France* hath craftily deceived us touching our territory of *Gafcoine*, wickedly detaining it from us, and now, not content with the fraud and wickednefs aforefaid, hath prepared a very great fleet, with a powerful army for the affaulting our kingdom, with which he hath already hoftilely invaded our kingdom, and the inhabitants of the faid kingdom, the *Englifh* tongue, if power correfpond with the deteftable purpofe of the conceived iniquity, which God avert, he purpofeth entirely to abolifh. Becaufe therefore darts forefeen hurt lefs, and your greateft intereft, with that of your fellow citizens of the faid kingdom is herein concerned, We charge you in the faith and love by which ye are held unto Us, ftrictly injoining that on the Lords day next after the feaft of St. *Martin*, in the winter next enfuing, ye be perfonally prefent at *Weftminfter*, forewarning the prior and chapter of your church, the archdeacons, and all the clergy of your diocefe, caufing that the faid prior and archdeacons in their own perfons, and

" procuratores

" procuratores idoneos plenam &
" fufficientem poteftatem ab ipfis
" capitulo & cleris habentes una
" vobifcum interfint modis omni-
" bus tunc ibidem ad tractandum
" ordinandum & faciendum nobif-
" cum & cum ceteris prelatis &
" proceribus et aliis incolis regni
" noftri qualiter fic hujufmodi peri-
" culis & ex cogitatis maliciis ob-
" viandum. Tefte rege apud Wen-
" geham tricefimo die Septem-
" bris."

the faid chapter by one, and alfo the clergy by two fit proctors having full and fufficient power from them the chapter and clergy, be prefent, together with you, by all ways then and there to confult, ordain, and take fuch effectual meafures, with us, and with the other prelates, and nobles and other inhabitants of our kingdom, as will obviate fuch dangers and malicious devices. Witnefs the king at *Wengeham*, the thirty-firft day of September.

That the right of reprefentation in parliament hath in other cafes been allowed, in confequence of the enlargement of the public territory. *Wales* was conquered by *Edward* I. by the ftat. of *Rutland* it was annexed to *England*; but their clofe, firm and perfect union was made by the ftat. 27. *Hen.* VIII. cap. 25. wherein it is recited that " Albeit " the dominion, principality, and country of *Wales* juftly and right- " eoufly was, and ever had been incorporated, annexed, united, and fub- " ject to and under the *Imperial* crown of this realm, as a very member " and joint of the fame;" and yet, from certain caufes therein mentioned, " fome rude and ignorant people had made diftinction and " diverfity between the kings fubjects of this realm, and his fubjects " of the faid dominion and principality of *Wales*, whereby great " difcord, variance, debate, divifion, murmur, and fedition had grown " between his faid fubjects;" wherefore, among other reafons, " to " bring his faid fubjects of this his realm, and of his faid dominion of " *Wales* to an amicable concord and unity," among other things, provifion was made for its reprefentation in parliament. And the firft *Englifh* colony having been planted at *Calais*, the fame parliament, in the fame feffion, provided for its reprefentation in parliament alfo. The firft writ thereupon iffued, that I have feen, bears date the 2d day of Auguft, in the firft year of the reign of *Edward* VI. whereby the king

12 Edw. I.

commanded

commanded the mayor and burgeffes to caufe to be elected a difcreet inhabitant of the faid borough, to be a burgefs for his parliament for the fame, according to the form of an act made by the parliament held the 27th *Hen*. VIII. aforementioned; " fo that the faid burgefs fhould have " full and fufficient power for himfelf and the faid community to do " and confent to what fhould be ordained by the common council of his " kingdom."

VI. That where religion, liberty, order, and good government are, there will be numbers, plenty, ftrength and fafety, with a proper union of all the parts for the good of the whole—That as the declenfion and diffolution of fo many different ftates irrefiftably prove the difficulty of perpetual prefervation, fo it is likewife certain that commercial and naval empires are unavoidably attended with fpecial difficulties refpecting their duration and flourifhing condition. For proof of this we need not have recourfe to the ancients, *Europe* having within thefe three hundred years given us fo many examples, that it would be tedious as well as unneceffary and unpleafant to compare their prefent with their former ftate.—That commerce when fhe takes her flight leaves a country in a worfe condition than fhe found it, and knowing no return, the inhabitants may in vain lament that lofs which their improvidence or unkind ufage caufed.—That although ftrength be ever preferable to wealth, yet when the ftate is greatly infected by luxury, whofe natural offspring are diffipation, folly, fraud, diftrefs, and danger, with mental enervation, which united, with or without concomitant caufes, have fo often occafioned diffolution or deftruction, greater attention is paid to thofe trades and traders which minifter to luxury, and weaken the ftate, than to thofe which ftrengthen it. Of this we have given the world a memorable example. What a ftir do we from time time make about the *Eaft India* trade, not to mention others, which never raifed the feamen it deftroys, and promotes luxury fo many different ways, while we pay fuch a difproportionate regard to the trade with and of our colonies, which, including the fifheries, to ufe the naval expreffion of an intelligent friend, is the main ftay of the *Britifh* commerce; fo that although trade be in its nature fo intricate and delicate that human wifdom, even after the ftricteft enquiry into facts, is frequently unequal to the difficulty

of

of forming falutary regulations for it, inftead of clofe attention, examination and comprehenfion, we are fometimes inclined, even on great
occafions, to confide in the fpecious and erroneous reprefentation of
others, who make a parade of their knowledge in thofe fubjects to feveral of whofe effential parts they are utter ftrangers—That our foreign
trade collectively confidered hath declined apace, and that depending on
the changeable minds and circumftances of other princes and ftates,
they are in effect contending various ways for its farther diminution, our
colony trade having in the mean time fo far encreafed as to have exceeded all thefe diminutions, and while profecuting to the utmoft by the
fpirit of the colonifts, who employed herein all their ftock and domeftic
credit, with a large credit given by the *Britifh* merchants, and when
labouring under various difficulties, a project was formed of raifing a
revenue upon it, with the traders and other inhabitants—That to carry
on a general trade a proportionate ftock of money is requifite ; and when
this project was formed there was in the continent colonies fcarcely
money fufficient, even with the aid of the paper currency ufed by feveral, to carry on their trade—That the money propofed to be raifed
by way of revenue being to be collected from the old and principal trad-
ing colonies, and wholly, or chiefly fpent upon new and diftant acquifi-
tions, the execution of this project muft of neceffity diminifh and em-
barrafs their trade, to the prejudice of the trade of this kingdom, all
the real money then remaining in the continent colonies probably amount-
ing to about an eighth or tenth part of what was due from the traders
there to the *Britifh* merchants, and which being fuffered to remain there
as the neceffary means of driving about the wheels of trade would affift
the traders in the difcharge of their debts, and in the continuance of
that large trade which they have fo long carried on for the common
benefit—That in a country dependant on commerce the primary object
of political confideration relative to it is prefumed to be the increafe and
exports of its manufactures, the benefits whereof are diffufed through
all parts; and therefore raifing a revenue upon their diminution is in
effect making a dangerous ftroke at the root of that which ought to be
cherifhed, or proceeding like him who cut the bough whereon he ftood
—That the colonies, fuppofing the annual exports of *Britifh* commodities

ties to them to amount to the value of two millions sterling, have thereby
probably paid yearly one million of the *British* taxes, or considerably
more.   To illustrate this particular, it is to be observed that every manu-
facturer charges all the taxes paid by him upon his manufacture.   A clo-
thier for instance who employs a thousand persons, whose taxes, together with those of his own family, amount to £ 10000, he being reim-
bursed by the sale of his cloth, each piece bears of course its proportion of
the whole, and is paid finally by the wearer.   The amount of the public
demands are by the intelligent variously estimated.   An old friend, who
in many respects is extremely acute in his discernment touching the in-
teriour state of the kingdom, as well as exact in his calculations, and
who by the way had hard measure in one of our late ministerial revo-
lutions, some time before the commencement of the last war mentioned
to me with approbation an estimate made with diligence by other judicious persons, whereby it was supposed that the same amounted to fourteen shillings in the pound; so that according to this calculate the accu-
mulative part of the price of manufactures in proportion to the natural
is as fourteen to six.   Being no competent judge of all the particulars
of this affair, I leave them to those who are; but taking the lowest
estimates of the amount of the British exports to the colonies, and of the
public charges, through various circulations resting on them, and finally
on their consumers, and considering the same together with the entire
commercial and pecuniary state of the colonies, it clearly appears to me
that this revenue-project, if peaceably carried into execution, as far as
the nature of things would permit, would by its natural operations certainly have caused so great a diminution in the exports of *British* commodities that for every penny collected in the colonies by way of revenue this kingdom would very soon have lost six-pence, and probably
in a short time considerably more.   The history of commerce fully
proves that it cannot be preserved without consulting its nature, with
all its connections, and trade will sometimes, like water, only bear its
own weight, and the trade of the colonies having been strained to the
utmost, and its products collected from all parts constantly leaving the
traders there immensely in debt to the *British* merchants, its continuance was incompatible with new burthens, and the application of that

money

money to other purposes which was neceſſary to carry it on—that the moſt judicious perſons have in time paſt thought it adviſeable by every proper method to encreaſe the trade of the colonies, keeping it under due regulations, and to aſſiſt in providing for them ſuch profitable employment as might enable them to pay for large quantities of *Britiſh* manufactures; whereas this new project hath a direct tendency to drive the inhabitants out of trade, and from the ſea coaſt into the inland parts of the country, where every man living upon his freehold will eat his own mutton, and cloath himſelf with the ſkin and the wool.—That the colonies, like this and other countries, animated by the ſpirit of trade, would as they encreaſed their ability, as they have in times paſt, continue to encreaſe their trade, and diſtreſſing this trade with the traders is ſtarving the hen that lays the golden egg.—That the cheriſhing and regulating is ſo far preferable to the impoveriſhing ſyſtem, that there is not a political truth, even that which declares honeſty to be the beſt policy, that appears more clear to me than this, That the flouriſhing trade and condition of the colonies will ever beſt ſecure and augment their commercial and beneficial connection with this kingdom. By their nature and original ſettlement they are unqueſtionably part of the family of *England*, and their comfortable condition will not only enable them to proſecute trade in time of peace, but invigorate their defence in time of war, of which it is not improbable they may again be the ſeat. There is no end of vulgar errors relative to this particular; our enemies attack our colonies as eſſential parts of that commercial and naval empire which they would reduce; and if, inſtead of promoting and ſtrengthning the moſt deſirable union, our errors and theirs, with conſequent diviſions, ſhould make them more vulnerable, they will of courſe become the object of the enemies policy and force; and, lamenting our diviſions conſidered in every light, I am ſorry that ſome of our politicians have not been enclined to ſuch treatment of them, that, to uſe the words of a worthy patriot, ſpoken to the king on the throne, it might be their inclination as well as duty to be obedient to his majeſty and the laws. On the other hand it behoves the colonies to conſider that their honour and their intereſt, their ſafety and happineſs conſiſt in their continuing proper and uſeful members of the

common-

common-wealth, to take care that the fpirit of liberty be accompanied with a due fenfe of government; to maintain their rights and interefts in proper manner, and to pay the fame reverence to the king and the parliament as if placed nearer to them, remembring what was faid by an author whofe credit they will not queftion [*l*], " this is not the " liberty which we can hope, that no grievance ever fhould arife in the " commor-wealth; that let no man in this world expect; but when " complaints are freely heard, deeply confidered, and fpeedily reformed, " then is the utmoft bound of civil liberty attained, that wife men look " for."   And it may not be improper for others as well as the colonifts on this occafion to recollect not only the faying of *Vopifcus*, but like-wife the words of the judicious Dr. *Fleetwood*.   " The prefent defigns " of men have, it may be, no eye or tendency to fuch and fuch a confe-" quence; but, however, men muft look to it; for when we are once " out of the right way, every ftep we take leads us but into farther " wanderings; and we know not whither we are going."

VII. With refpect to the reafons relative to the repeal of the ftamp-act, extraneous to the real merits of the cafe, I fhall not prefume to ex-prefs my own fentiments; but, under favour, fhall infert the words of Mr. *Milton*, in his *Areopagitica*, addreffed to the parliament of *England*, wherein, after taking notice that there were abundant examples of pri-vate perfons giving their counfel by fpeech or writing to fundry free ftates, in thofe ages to whofe polite wifdom and letters we owe that we are not *Goths* and *Jutlanders*, he wrote thus; " and how far you excel " them, be affured, Lords and Commons. there can no greater tefti-" mony appear, than when your prudent fpirit acknowledges and obeys " the voice of reafon, from what quarter foever it be heard fpeaking; " and renders ye as willing to repeal any act of your own fetting forth, " as any fet forth by your predeceffors."   And fhall obferve that in feveral countries ruled by abfolute princes an appeal lies from the de-cree of the prince, that is, *à fe male informato, ad fe bene informatum*; and I have ever underftood that the honour of the prince was more

[*l*] Mr. *Milton*.

concerned

concerned in giving a juft decree upon the appeal and review of the cafe, than in pronouncing his firft decree.

As to thofe fons of violence who, without taking notice of others, have to the diſhonour of that colony whofe merits with refpect to its mother country, all things confidered, exceed thofe of any one of an hundred *Roman* colonies, not to name a greater number, have rifen up in its capital, and, under the pretence of reformation, have committed fuch outrages, I exhort every man of them, for his own fake, as well as that of others, that leaving the care of the common rights to thofe to whom it belongs, and renouncing his offences, he continue to be quiet, and by his peaceable and proper behaviour prepare himfelf to partake of the clemency of a gracious prince who delights in the exercife of his mercy. And, in order to mollify the minds of thofe who feem as great ftrangers to humanity as they are to found policy, I fhall, in the words of *Lipfius*, fet forth the mild conduct of an excellent prince.

" Shall I omit thee *Alphonfus?* who being all goodnefs and benefience " haft reprefented to us *Titus*, but with long continuance. Thou be- " fieging *Caieta*, which had obftinately rebelled againft thee, the befieged " appeared to be preffed with want of provifions, which themfelves de- " clared by putting forth old men, boys, women, and all the ufelefs " multitude. In council it was advifed that they fhould be rejected and " driven back, for that fo the city would foon furrender, he through com- " miferation chofe rather to difmifs them, and continue the fiege : but, " upon his not taking the place, fome dared to object, that if he had not let " them go the city would have been his; he nobly anfwered. *But the fafe-* " *ty of fo many perfons, is more to me than an hundred Caietas.* However he " was not long without it, for the citizens, admonifhed by fuch extra- " ordinary virtue, and repenting, voluntarily furrendered themfelves. " His conduct was fimilar towards *Anthony Caldora*, the moft powerful " man of the *Neapolitan* kingdom, and his obftinate enemy, whom hav- " ing at length in a great battle fubdued, and taken, when all perfuaded " to put to death fo troublefome a man, and who was ever at enmity " with the *Arragonians*, he alone withftood, and not only pardoned, but " reftored his eftate to him, and gave to his wife all his elegant and " valuable furniture and other moveables, which he had in his hands,

" referving

" reserving to himself only one cryſtal cup. Such were his actions,
" with which his expreſſions accorded. Being aſked why he was mild
" towards all, even the wicked. *Becauſe*, ſaid he, *juſtice conciliateth the*
" *good, clemency the bad.* Again, when his miniſters complained of his
" too great lenity, as not becoming a prince. *What*, ſaid he, *would you*
" *have bears and lions to reign? For clemency is the peculiar of men,*
" *cruelty of wild beaſts.* He ſaid what was true. By how much the
" greater, and more, as I may ſay, of a man any one is, ſo much the
" more is he inclined to this virtue, which is therefore termed huma-
" nity."

Scotland in conſequence of two rebellions raiſed there, in order to
deſtroy, or drive away the preſent royal family, happily placed on the
throne for the preſervation of our common liberties, hath by the wiſdom
and equity of the *Britiſh* parliament been made more free, whereas the
end and intention of every action being to be conſidered, in juſtice to the
colonies, whoſe diſtance lays them under manifold difficulties, it may be
ſaid, if I am not wholly miſtaken, that their intention is to defend their
rights according to their ſenſe of them, and how far that is erroneous,
or its defence improper, is not my province to declare. As to theſe politicians who ſeem to delight in blood, and are ſo ſollicitous to introduce a
ſocial war, whereby after ſo narrowly eſcaping the ſword of our enemies
we ſhould employ our own ſwords in deſtroying ourſelves, every ſtab
deſtroying a ſubject, and diminiſhing that commerce which gives bread to
ſo many others, their policy, inſtead of being the reſult of any wiſe conſideration ſuitable to the occaſion, ſeems to be the dictates of their prejudice, their paſſions, or ſomething worſe. If theſe advocates for de-
ſtruction had been pleaſed fully to explain their own propoſition, conſidered with reſpect to its nature, operations, and concluſion, without which
all propoſals are vain, its impropriety and dangers, I preſume, would
evidently appear.

Rome when in her flouriſhing eſtate was brought to the brink of ruin
by the ſocial war, occaſioned by her refuſal to communicate the *Roman*
right. After ſuffering ſo much by her various errors and corruptions
ſhe granted it to all the nations of which her empire was compoſed, and
                                                                    for

for this grant her praifes in verfe and profe will endure to all ages. *Claudian* fays,

> *Hæc eft in gremium victos quæ fola recepit,*
> *Humanumque genus communi nomine fovit,*
> *Matris, non dominæ, ritu : civefque vocavit*
> *Quos domuit, nexuque pio longinqua revinxit.*

And *Rutilius*,

> *Fecifti patriam diverfis gentibus unam,*
>   *Profuit injuftis te dominante capi.*
> *Dumque offers victis proprii confortia juris,*
>   URBEM *fecifti quod prius* ORBIS *erat.*

Upon taking a view of all parts of the public territory, and confidering them in their nature, fituation and mutual relations, with the relation of the whole to other ftates, including our debts, which all the money in *Europe* probably could not difcharge, whereof the principal or intereft due to foreigners is to be paid by the balance of our trade, and how far our credit is exhaufted, together with the ordinary courfe of human affairs refpecting war and peace, it does not, I prefume, require the forefight of *Themiftocles* to difcern that our future welfare and fafety require the prefent exercife of great wifdom ; and that the whole having one common intereft to fupport againft our competitors, adverfaries and enemies, and all being members of the fame body, laying afide our prejudices, divifions and animofities, we fhould unite our endeavours for the advancement of the common good, ever remembring that juftice is an architectonic virtue, and what we learn from *Æfop*, and that wife and great emperour and philofopher *Antoninus*, that the bundle of fticks given by the father to his fons while united is not to be broken, and that what is not good for the hive is not good for the bee ; and moreover what was faid to the Lords and Commons in Parliament, *Eritis infuperabiles, fi fueritis infeparabiles. Explofum eft illud* 4 Hen. VI. *diverbium: Divide & impera ; cùm radix & vertex imperii in obedientium confenfu rata fint.*

Having

Having for the advancement of truth, liberty, univerſal juſtice, and the public welfare, ſubjeċts worthy of a much abler pen, written with that freedom which becomes the member of a free ſtate, I ſhall now cheer-fully ſubmit the whole to the candour and correċtion of the judicious and impartial, and to the pleaſure of thoſe who delight in cenſure. With reſpeċt to the former I ſhall ever ſay bleſſed be the amending hand, and of the latter I pray this favour, that they will for the common good be pleaſed to write better on theſe important ſubjeċts.

F I N I S.

E R R A T A.

p.	l.	
1	4	dele the comma after *affairs*.
17	16	read, *judicially*.
42		dele the inverted commas from the 9th to the 14th line.
49	7	read, *in forming*.
54	21	read, *commonly*.
58	21	read, *freehold*.
97	22	read, *attaching*.
99	23	read, *commiſſion*.
		From p. 104, to 113, read, 105, &c.
117,		laſt line but two, read, *on*.
119	32	read, *feruntur*.
143		laſt line, read *immutable*.